VENTUREBALL

VENTUREBALL

THE ART OF WINNING IN PROFESSIONAL SPORTS BY INNOVATING OUTSIDE THE LINES

SEAN HOFFMAN

NEW DEGREE PRESS

VENTUREBALL

The Art of Winning in Professional Sports By Innovating Outside the Lines

ISBN   978-1-64137-163-6   *Paperback*

978-1-64137-164-3   *Ebook*

To my Dad, who is no longer the only published author in the family.

CONTENTS

INTRODUCTION

———

"Innovation is taking two things that already exist and putting them together in a new way."

—TOM FRESTON

March 27, 2012, was a huge day for any Dodgers fan.

That was the day an ownership group led by NBA Hall of Famer Magic Johnson and former Atlanta Hawks president Stan Kasten purchased the baseball team for a record-breaking $2 billion. This deal was big news. Not because Magic Johnson now owned a LA sports team. Not because it was the highest amount paid for a sports franchise ever. But because it ended the disastrous relationship between the Dodgers and their former owner, Frank McCourt.

When McCourt owned the team from 2004 to 2012, he used the Dodgers as collateral to fund his luxurious lifestyle, purchasing mansions and extravagant cars for him and his wife. The Dodgers' financial performance took a hard hit; the team was losing money left and right. As a result, McCourt struggled to fund the Dodgers' expensive payroll—which ranked fourth highest among MLB team payrolls in 2003—forcing him to ship off star players, such as Shawn Green and his $14 million-per-year contract, to other teams for cheaper assets. In just two seasons after McCourt purchased the team, the Dodgers' team payroll dropped over $20 million and fell from the top-10 highest payroll list for the first time since 1996.

To make matters worse, McCourt went through a very public divorce, during which his former wife, Jamie McCourt, claimed she owned 50% of the team while McCourt asserted he owned all of it. Court battles ensued, and the attention quickly shifted away from the Dodgers' on-field performance to the court room. Fearing that he could no longer finance the payroll of the team, McCourt filed for bankruptcy protection in 2011, solidifying the Dodgers' status as the laughingstock of the league.

Fortunately for the Dodgers, this fiasco had a Hollywood ending with McCourt agreeing to put the team up for sale in 2012.

But once the Dodgers were sold by the McCourts, the new ownership group knew they had a tall task at hand.

How could they recapture the value lost by poor management?

* * *

Perhaps it shouldn't be surprising that sports, tech, startups, and venture capital intersect in the ways that they have.

Each represents an aspect of the world that is aspirational, ambitious, and desired by the masses. Who wouldn't want to be a part of a professional sports team? What could be better than utilizing technologies spanning from virtual reality to artificial intelligence, and from the internet of things to synthetic biology? Who doesn't wish they could be the founder of today's most iconic startups such as Facebook, Uber, Spotify, or Airbnb—or if you can't be the founder, then why not be the venture capitalist who invested in them?

Startups.

Sports.

A match made in heaven—and it's perhaps why Joe Lacob, the majority owner of the Golden State Warriors who won three NBA titles in four years, sits at the intersection of these two industries.

Lacob worked in venture capital for three decades, building a reputation as a winner from his time at Silicon Valley giant Kleiner Perkins.

And not only do the sports teams' owners bring venture and startup savvy to the sports world, but athletes have also begun to do the same, with retired NBA stars like Kobe Bryant launching $100 million venture funds and current stars like Kevin Durant choosing to play in the Bay Area partly so he can explore business opportunities centered in Silicon Valley.

Startups and sports are becoming forever linked.

So, perhaps it should not surprise us that the link is not just theoretical.

* * *

The new ownership of the Dodgers had a problem.

The team they'd purchased for a hefty sum had poor front office leadership and had lost many of its star assets that previously made it the envy of the league.

The new owners had ample history in entrepreneurship and understood its value to corporate innovation. They decided to put money into something that would surprise many in the sports world:

Startups.

Using the group's knowledge and experience in the field, Dodgers Chief Financial Officer Tucker Kain had the perfect idea to support continuous innovation: the introduction of an accelerator program for tech startups.

Dubbing this new initiative the Dodgers Accelerator Program, the team began accepting mature-staged tech start-ups in 2015, becoming the first professional sports team to introduce such a program.

The shift toward better management translated to performance on the field as well. A year after the ownership change, the Dodgers' payroll returned to its high roller status, fielding the second-highest team payroll in 2013 with $213 million. The Dodgers rediscovered their on-field excellence, winning five straight division titles from 2013 to 2017, capped off by a World Series appearance in 2017.

* * *

I didn't know much about the Dodgers' success in innovating off the field; I just knew that their young players started to become the types of people that I'd follow, see featured on SportsCenter, and pick in my fantasy baseball drafts.

The Dodgers were back, but their link to startups? Not even on my radar.

It was the summer of 2017, just a few short months before I would be living with four of my best friends.

But the excitement was halted by an email from our campus housing office just a month before we moved in, saying that a spot in our apartment had opened up—we were no longer five.

- Did two of my roommates have a falling out?
- Did one of my roommates transfer without telling us?
- Did one of my roommates drop out?

I immediately texted the group chat. "What's up with that email? Is everyone ok?"

"Yeah what's the deal? Who's leaving?" another one of my friends sent.

After a stressful five minutes of silence, we finally got an answer.

"Oh yeah totally forgot to tell you guys, I'm not going to be at school next year," the friend texted.

"Ummmm what?"

"The 76ers invested in my company so I'm moving up to Philadelphia for the year to work in their accelerator program."

And just like that, Dylan Elder, one of the goofiest kids I know, pulled a Mark Zuckerberg, putting his education on hold to pursue his passion project.

Sports teams are investing in startups?

Hmmm, I thought.

* * *

Sports have been a part of my life ever since I was a little kid. Whether it was playing or watching them, every day of my childhood seemed to involve sports. Once I realized I had no shot at becoming a professional athlete, I expanded my interests. My passion for startups was sparked by an entrepreneurship class I took in high school, but I never married the two interests together—that is, until I learned of an amazing opportunity presented to my friend Dylan.

In fact, Dylan never made it to a class that year. He was too busy working on his startup, Monster Roster, in Philadelphia under the Philadelphia 76ers' newly formed accelerator—appropriately named the Sixers Innovation Lab.

Due to my budding interest in entrepreneurship, I would ask Dylan question after question about his experiences working in an accelerator:

- Do you have any other investors?
- What is Monster Roster's valuation?
- Have you gotten offers from Fanduel or Draftkings yet?

I was incredibly jealous, mainly because I did not have a startup of my own to apply to one of these programs, but also because Dylan was part of an emerging trend that I had zero prior knowledge about: professional sports teams investing in startups.

This phenomenon certainly begs the question: Why?

In today's society, where technology is easily accessible, companies are constantly looking for ways to innovate. Corporate innovation is a top priority for large companies looking to gain a competitive edge and increase their market share. In his book *The Startup Way,* entrepreneur Eric Ries discusses his experiences working with executives at top corporations, stressing the importance of promoting corporate innovation through "entrepreneurial management." Ries believes the best way to innovate is to think like an entrepreneur and install a culture shift throughout the company to promote creativity and "continuous innovation."

Yet instituting a drastic shift in thinking within a large corporation could be quite a challenge. There will always be bottlenecks who slow down the process, or straight-up refuse to be a part of it.

Now, take a look at professional sports teams.

In an industry that has remained relatively constant since the early 20th century, professional sports teams used to compete primarily for on-field dominance. But as the amount of money invested into each franchise increases year after year, so too does the expectation of sizable financial returns. And, because only one team can win it all every year, teams are always looking for more ways to differentiate themselves to add value to their brand and gain that competitive edge, whether it be on or off the field.

The 76ers were *not the first pro team to find value in investing in startups.*

That honor belongs to the Los Angeles Dodgers, who underwent a dramatic shift in team ownership that guided them back to the top of the league.

* * *

This book is designed to show you why *every consumer brand will eventually be investing in or acquiring innovative startups and young companies.*

Perhaps it makes sense why sports was one of the first industries to embrace startup investment in this manner—but don't be surprised to see a future in which it's the norm in everything from mining and automotive to the federal government and aviation.

Inside the book, you'll hear a variety of unique stories, including how:

- the Philadelphia 76ers took a gamble on a college freshman's startup idea
- the Washington Capitals used investments in sports technology on their way to capturing the team's first Stanley Cup

- LeBron James' investment helped a pizza joint become the fastest growing restaurant chain in U.S. history
- sports organizations are preparing for the future of eSports
- individual athletes are identifying and exploiting gaps in existing markets to start their own companies

* * *

The Dodgers' story demonstrates how startups are the key driver in disruptive technology and perhaps the best way for corporations to gain a competitive edge through strategic partnerships and investments. In this book, you'll discover how sports teams and individual athletes are getting involved in startups, not only to achieve innovation but also to strive for continuous innovation to increase their brand's value over time.

You do not need to be a sports fan to read this book. Honestly, you can read this book even if you've never watched a sports game. The lessons learned from the workings of athletes and owners can be applied to executives at corporations in any industry looking to employ a different strategy regarding corporate innovation. And if you happen to be an entrepreneur working on the next big thing, just know there are plenty of opportunities to find investors within companies if you present your idea in the right manner.

No matter what field you're an expert in, innovation remains a key factor in determining success. By learning how to effectively identify and incorporate disruptive technology through startups into your company, you can expect great returns through corporate innovation.

CHAPTER 1

UNDERSTANDING CORPORATE INNOVATION MODELS

———

"You don't skate to where the puck is. You want to skate to where the puck is going to be."

—WAYNE GRETZKY.

$1,000,000,000.

One trillion dollars.

That was the goal.

The question?

Who would get there first.

In a fight with Amazon over market valuation, Apple came out the winner, becoming the first American company in history to reach a $1 trillion in value on August 2, 2018. In a world full of Apple products, it was only a matter of time that they reached this milestone. However, Apple would have never gotten to this point without the introduction of one innovative product back in 2001: the iPod.

In 1997, Apple looked far from the tech giant it has grown to today. On August 6, 1997, Microsoft essentially bailed Apple out with a $150 million investment. But, that was not the true turning point for Apple's resurgence. Apple's return to the to top of the technology industry is attributed to the return of their founder, Steve Jobs, and his reinstatement as CEO in July 1997.

Before the iPod, Sony was the main pioneer in how people consumed music, with the introduction of the Sony Walkman in 1979, allowing customers to listen to their cassette tapes on the go. Over time, the walkman adjusted to the changes in the music consumption, developing Walkmans for CDs.

But Jobs saw the bigger picture. Not only did Jobs want to change the way people listened to music, but he also wanted to change the way people *purchased their music.*

Throughout the product development of the iPod, Jobs met with record labels, persuading them to agree to a new licensing and sales model for music that would support the iPod. Instead of having customers constantly changing the CDs and cassettes they were listening to on their Walkmans, Jobs envisioned users purchasing music on a digital market space and downloading them straight to the device.

After getting the record labels to agree with his new business model, Jobs successfully built an ecosystem for the iPod from the ground up, ensuring that this product will disrupt how people listen to their music. With that, the iTunes Store was born.

Following the release of the iPod was the introduction of the iPhone, marrying your cell phone with your personal music device. Then came the iPad. Then the Apple Watch.

And the music ecosystem has also drastically changed. Traditional methods of music consumption, such as cassettes and CDs, have become obsolete thanks to digital streaming services such as Apple Music and Spotify.

All because of one, *innovative product. The iPod.*

* * *

Innovation.

Perhaps the most popular buzzword in the business community nowadays.

It seems as if every company is boasting about "innovative" products in development or recruiting "innovative" individuals to be their next employees.

And, yet, the rise of popularity in use of the word has made it increasingly difficult to reach a consensus on the definition of innovation.

The idea of innovation is best encapsulated by the aforementioned Gretzky quote. As a corporation, it is not your goal to get to where your competition already is, whether its in terms of market share, sales growth, or product development.

Instead, innovation is about getting to where your competition *will be, and attempting to reach that status before your competitors do. Steve Jobs envisioned the trend of digital music consumption and decided to implement a product that supports this notion, as well as a digital, internal marketplace, to turn this vision into a reality. And he did this before his competition.*

According to the Oxford dictionary, innovation is defined as "the introduction of new things, ideas, or ways of doing something".

For the sake of this book, I am using the textbook definition of innovation and applying it to the business world. My definition of innovation is the introduction of new business operations aimed to provide an existing corporation with a competitive advantage. Innovation is doing something that your competitors are not.

I've purposely left the definition of innovation vague, as it can be applied across all industries and what constitutes innovation varies among different industries. Something as simple as a squeezable ketchup bottle could be viewed as innovative in the food industry, but companies in the automative industry require 'bigger picture' innovations, such as the introduction of electric cars.

* * *

As seen in the Apple example, innovation is necessary for business to survive. As technology has become more and more accessible, consumers' expectations for businesses have grown. A 2015 Harris Poll survey of 300 U.S. corporate executives at companies with revenues larger than $1 billion reported that 82% of executives believe that their customers have higher expectations than they did three years ago. When asked a follow-up question of how rising customer expectations have affected their companies' goals and objectives, 65% of executives reported back an increased pressure to innovate.

Data from Innosight, an innovation consulting firm, supports the need for corporate innovation, reporting that the average lifespan of an S&P 500 company is declining. During the 1990s, the average lifespan hovered around 25 years, compared to 2017's average lifespan of 20 years. The trend is projected to decline in the future, dipping below 15 years in 2022, further demonstrating the importance of innovation in today's existing markets.

But not every company can be as successful as Apple. While Apple relied heavily on their research & development team for the iPod, that does not mean that is the best way for a company to innovate. Companies operate differently, and manage innovation in various ways. The six basic corporate innovation models are:

1. Research and Development
2. Incubators

3. Accelerators
4. Venture Capitalists
5. Mergers and Acquisitions
6. Partnerships

Each of the corporate innovation models can be distinguished in two buckets, internal innovation and external innovation, categorized by who has control over the "innovation assets", defined by the Preseident of Touchdown Venture, Scott Lenet, as the ideas, technology, inventions, business models, and legal entities attached to innovation projects.

Research and Development

Research and development is perhaps the most traditional corporate innovation model as companies have invested in internal R&D departments for over 50 years. With R&D, innovation starts in-house, with research, and remains internal, with development, throughout the process. The corporation maintains control over all innovation assets within the R&D team.

Incubators

Similar to R&D, corporate incubators rely heavily on internal innovation, starting with their employees. Within the general model of a corporate incubator, ideas are generated internally by select individuals, developed within the corporation, and then spun out either to be acquired by another corporation or to exist as its own entity.

Because incubators require large investments on the parent company's part, the incubator often receives equity ownership on par with start-up founders' stakes. Notable corporate incubators include Amazon Labs, responsible for the launch of Kindle, Echo, and Fire products, and Google's Foundry, an offshoot of Google's secretive R&D department X.

The corporation managing the incubator maintains full control over the innovation assets until the new company is ready to exist as its own entity.

Accelerators

While both R&D and incubators are examples of internal innovation, accelerators are an example of external innovation. Unlike incubators, accelerators focus on recruiting existing startups to bring in-house and provide them with benefits such as mentorship, legal services, fundraising advice, product development, and sometimes even capital investments.

The main difference between an incubator and an accelerator is that startups must apply to participate within a corporate accelerator program. Since accelerators are a source of external innovation, corporations maintain limited control of a startup's innovation assets while participating in the program. However, depending on the legal terms of the accelerator program, corporations could maintain limited control over innovation assets even after a startup has graduated from the program.

Venture Capitalists

Another example of an external innovation model, corporate venture capitalists focus on identifying mature startups and invest a minority equity stake in the startup. The size of the stake depends on the amount of the investment, the stage of the startup, and other external market factors.

The corporation maintains limited control over the innovation assets of the startup from the time of the initial investment until an exit sale, and the influence of the venture capitalist varies depending on the terms of the investment.

Mergers and Acquisitions

Perhaps the most basic form of external innovation, mergers and acquisitions occur when a larger corporation buys out startups or other smaller companies to bring their innovation assets internally. Once the corporation purchases the startup, it gains full control of all innovation assets.

Partnerships

Partnerships are another form of external innovation that focuses on utilizing an existing startups' innovation assets with minimal levels of investment. Partnerships involves negotiating a deal allowing a larger corporation access to a startup's technology or product.

Usually, partnerships do not involve an exchange for equity in the startup, therefore keeping the control of the innovation assets within the startup, not the corporation.

* * *

Trends in corporate innovation have drastically changed since the turn of the century. While R&D may have been the saving grace for Apple in the 1990s and early 2000s, innovation consultants believe R&D is not as effective as other means of innovation.

Tendayi Viki, a manging partner at Benneli Jacobs, is one of those critics, pointing to a 2017 study done by Strategy& which concluded that there is no correlation between R&D spending and sales growth.

While R&D helped Apple introduce the innovative iPod in 2001 and led to an increase in the company's global revenue, recently the tech giant's R&D spending has shown little to no correlation to the company's sales. In 2005, Boston Consulting Group labeled Apple as the "most innovative company in the world". That year, Apple experienced an 68.3% increase in revenue and only increased its investment into R&D by 9.2%. Conversely, in 2016 Apple's revenue declined by 7.7% compared to the previous period, but R&D investment increased by 25%. An issue with R&D spending is that pumping money into the department does not always translate to innovation and revenue growth. Increased spending in R&D leads to the risk of stifling innovation, wrongly prioritizing the completion of new projects to achieve one-time innovation, rather than working to improve existing products and introducing new technologies to position the firm for continuous innovation.

Viki later supports this argument by introducing the idea that the goal of innovation is to solve for both market risk, whether or not consumers will purchase this product, and technology risk, is the company able to develop new technologies that work. Viki argues that R&D focuses only on technology risks, not market risks, and provides an innovation equation:

Innovation = invention + customer value + business model

The invention aspect of the equation addresses technology risks, while customer value and business model represent the market risks that are trying to be solved.

The launch of the iPod did not solely succeed on the basis of technology behind the invention, but succeeded because Jobs also sought to enhance the customer value by providing them with a better portable music playing device and a digital marketplace to support the business model.

Deborah Weinswig, an expert in the retail industry, is the CEO and founder of Coresight Research, a think tank that explores the intersection of retail and technology to provide business advice on corporate innovation. Weinswig shares Viki's beliefs, supporting the notion that corporate innovation through dedicated corporate innovation centers, such as accelerators and incubators, is replacing R&D.

Weinswig explores the emerging trend of an "open model" for corporate innovation, in which companies are innovating externally through accelerators, incubators, and/or partnerships in her report, *Deep Dive: The Evolution of Corporate Innovation*. Weinswig presents the argument that retailers are adopting open innovation strategies as they facilitate an accelerated speed of innovation, allows for more collaboration with external partners, and often requires less capital requirements than in-house R&D departments.

An open model for corporate innovation often accelerates the pace of innovation, compared to R&D, due to their ability to operate as a single entity from the parent corporation. While in-house R&D departments must follow directions and constraints provided by the corporation, accelerator and incubator programs allow for faster prototyping with fewer constraints.

Retail giants such as Walmart, Staples, and Target have implemented shifts in their approach to innovation, introducing their own corporate innovation centers. Staples successfully launched Staples Velocity Lab in 2012, recruiting current employees and external e-commerce and IT experts to join the team. With a fresh outside perspective coupled with veteran employees who understood the brand, Staples Velocity Lab successfully launched a digital wallet service in just nine weeks, and, according to a company report, was Staples' fastest deployment of a project ever.

In 2016, Target partnered with TechStars to create a retail-oriented accelerator program; the retailer has continued to work with startups post-accelerator graduation, such as by investing in Inspectorio, an inspection software startup dedicated to improving product quality assurance.

But, as Weinswig points out, retail is not the only industry experiencing this emerging trend. In July 2015, research firm

Altimeter released a report on innovation methods within the top 200 companies, by revenue, across five industries: automotive, financial services, consumer products/retail, manufacturing, and telecom. The initial study found that 38% of the 200 companies had established a corporate innovation model. A follow up study was conducted and reported that 67 new innovation centers opened between July 2015 and February 2016, and of the 67 new innovation centers, 55% of them operated as an accelerator program.

Because innovation is tied to customer's expectations of a brand, Weinswig conducted her own study to discover what corporations think their customers expect of them by selecting 20 retail companies that have opened innovation centers, including Nike and Walmart, to discover what areas of innovation they focus on. However, innovation centers do not have to be constrained by their area of focus, with many retailers reporting back more than one area of focus. Of the 20 retailers, 60% identified mobile technology to be among the focuses of their innovation centers, followed by 55% citing data analytics as an area of focus. Other areas of focus included 22% responding with payment technology and 19% identifying virtual/augmented reality.

While the sample size of the survey limits the reliability of the data, the results reflect a general trend among consumer buying habits. Consumers expect brands to match their wants and needs, and retailers have identified these areas as potential competitive advantages.

It is no coincidence that sports organizations who are participating in external corporate innovation are also focusing on these areas, especially mobile technology and data analytics. Retail consumers overlap with sports consumers, as well as the industry objectives themselves. Both the retail industry and sports industry attempt to sell experiences through products, whether its a brand new sneaker or a ticket to a regular season game, and organizations within those industries want to increase the perceived benefit of their offering through innovation.

Now that a basic framework of corporate models is laid out, I will now dive into how sports organizations are doing innovation right, through accelerator programs and strategic partnerships, while more and more individual athletes are grasping the idea of venture capitalists to expand the value of their personal brand.

CHAPTER 2

INNOVATION IN SPORTS

———

"Baseball people generally are allergic to new ideas. We are slow to change."

—BRANCH RICKEY

Baseball.

Coined "the national pastime" by the New York Mercury in 1856.

Throughout the 19th century, while the United States went through drastic changes ranging from the Civil War to the Industrial Revolution, the game of baseball, invented in 1839, remained a constant.

But being a "constant" is not enough. As the world changes, businesses must adapt along with it.

The MLB was the first of the current "Big Four" sports leagues (NBA, MLB, NFL, NHL) to be formed, with the establishment of the Cincinnati Red Stockings in 1869. However, the MLB would likely not exist today without the innovative thinking of key individuals who drove change.

Throughout much of the first half of the 20th century, the MLB as a league had an anti-innovation approach, largely due to its first league commissioner, former federal judge Kenesaw Mountain Landis, a strict traditionalist who valued the status quo. Many of the MLB practices we see today, such as night games, African-American players, and broadcasting deals, were heavily opposed by Commissioner Landis.

Fortunately for the MLB, a few individual team executives took matters into their own hands to fight the status quo and bring innovation to this stagnant league.

One of those individuals was Branch Rickey, who was the first to introduce two mainstays that are seen in the present-day MLB: the farm system and African-American players. During the 1910s, the St. Louis Cardinals were a "cash-poor" team struggling to attract talented players due to their inability to grant large contracts. To address this issue, Rickey began purchasing minor league teams, which allowed him exclusive rights to their players; the Cardinals thus no longer had to buy new players and saw financial gains by selling minor league players to other teams. The "farm system" that Rickey had created brought success to the Cardinals, who won four league championships between 1928 and 1934 after suffering three straight losing seasons from 1918 to 1920.

Rickey's innovative ideas did not end there. As general manager for the Brooklyn Dodgers, Rickey signed the first African-American baseball player, Jackie Robinson, despite the rest of the owners working on passing a resolution to ban the signing of African-Americans. Robinson immediately made an impact: In 1947 he took home the inaugural Rookie of the Year Award, which recognizes the best first-year player in the league.

Despite the success of both of Rickey's ideas, other teams were slow to adopt these practices. While the Cardinals quickly emerged as a perennial powerhouse, other teams did not begin to implement farm systems until 1932, when the New York Yankees implemented a system of their own. Ironically, the teams that refused to purchase minor league teams turned into persistent losers through the 1930s and 1940s. And, while Robinson took the league by storm, other teams remained wary of signing African-American players. It was not until 1959, when the Boston Red Sox signed Pumpsie

Green, that all existing MLB teams at the time broke their own color barrier.

Through these innovations, the talent level of the league increased, as well as the monetary value of each team, as attendance levels rapidly increased from 15 million in total season attendance in the 1950s to 72 million in 2017. Following the trend of attendance, the purchasing price for MLB teams grew exponentially, from under $100 million in 1970 to as much as $1.2 billion in 2017, the latter of which was the selling price for the Miami Marlins, the most recent team to change ownership.

In the modern digital age, innovation within sports leagues and organizations has become even more important as they attempt to adapt to the changing behaviors of their consumers, while also increasing their own value as a brand. Teams have shifted their focus to solving organizational issues through the intersection of sports and technology. Yet not every team practices innovation the same way. Throughout this book, I aim to lay out different practices of sports teams and their approaches to innovation.

* * *

Innovation in the professional sports industry requires identifying growing trends among its consumers and adapting policies to create a better environment for their fans. An example of this practice can be seen in the Miami NBA team.

Eric Woolworth, the president of business operations for the Miami Heat, outlined his organization's approach to innovation and stressed the importance of innovation.

"Absolutely," Woolworth responded when asked if it is equally as important for sports organizations to innovate like consumer product companies. "I will tell you that this industry is historically incredibly lazy when it comes to innovation. One of the areas we have invested a lot of time, effort, and money is in the mobile space. We built our mobile app [in 2015] while essentially other teams were waiting for someone to bring a mobile app to them."

Why mobile?

Because at the time of the app's release in 2015, 70% of U.S. adults had smartphones, according to Pew Research Center. Furthermore, mobile use surpassed desktop use in 2016, with StatCounter reporting that 51.3% of internet usage in 2016 was from a mobile or tablet device. Heat executives identified trends among their consumers and aimed to provide them with a more convenient method to purchasing tickets. Gone were the days of worrying if your paper tickets would arrive in the mail on time for the game and waiting in line to pick up tickets from will call. Now fans could purchase tickets and instantly download them to their smartphones.

Similarly to retailers, sports organizations are focusing their innovative approaches on mobile technology and payment services. Woolworth and the rest of his team understood the behavioral trends among consumers and provided Heat fans with new technologies to make their game-day experiences more convenient.

"We were the first NBA team to go completely mobile with our tickets and [are] trying to be cashless by the end of the year," Woolworth added.

Not only does the app benefit the fans, but it also allows the Heat to understand their consumers better, allowing them to utilize data analytics based on app usage.

"[The app] is driving incredible data capturing for us and addresses an issue that the industry has had in terms of knowing who is in our buildings and how they are behaving in our buildings," Woolworth explained.

For the Heat, the in-house development of the mobile app could be categorized under the research and development corporate innovation model. But, as previously mentioned, sports teams innovate differently depending on the style of the organization's ownership group.

Take the Dodgers, for example. As the first sports team to introduce an accelerator program, they admittedly took a huge risk in investing their resources into startups. While it is still early to determine the true success and return on investment of these programs, Woolworth remains skeptical about the experiment.

"Sports organizations that have gone in that direction are owned by these venture capitalist ownership groups that are naturally attracted to the idea of running multiple businesses and investing in startups," he said. "I think there's a danger when you put your folks that run your sports organizations to run tangential businesses. They take their eye off the ball, which is always going to be the prime sports organizations. So, you run the risk of becoming too thin in your management structure when you divert resources that would otherwise go towards selling tickets, sponsorship, and your core business to running these other startups that may or may not go anywhere."

Guggenheim Partners, an investment and advisory firm that currently holds an estimated $305 billion in assets, purchased the Dodgers from McCourt in 2012 and brought along a breadth of entrepreneurial-minded individuals with experience in investments. For a team owned by such individuals, implementing these accelerator programs made more sense.

Woolworth's opinion is shaped by the Miami Heat's ownership structure. Former Carnival Cruise CEO Micky Arison owns the Miami Heat and has been the majority owner and managing general partner for 22 years. Unlike the ownership of the Dodgers, Arison does not rely on outside investments and tangential businesses, instead focusing on the Miami Heat. And when the Heat does decide to venture into outside businesses, such as eSports, they do so in a low-risk manner.

As the popularity of eSports has increased over the past half-decade, so too has professional sports organizations' interest in involving themselves in the emerging industry. In September 2016, the Philadelphia 76ers became the first U.S. professional sports team to enter the eSports space, acquiring two eSports franchises, Team Dignitas and Team Apex, and combining them into one team under their control.

While mergers and acquisitions are one method for sports organizations to get involved in eSports teams, Woolworth shared how the Heat approached the eSports market differently.

"We are certainly curious, like everybody else, to see if there's something there. It could ultimately work in tandem with our core sports team in terms of facilities and the existing sales and marketing team we have here. But rather than invest a lot of money in a game that could be gone tomorrow, we entered in a partnership with an existing eSports company called Misfits," Woolworth explained. "We did a deal where we did not put any capital in, but we take on marketing and sales responsibility for a piece of the upside. We are in it, but without any skin in the game."

Ted Leonsis, former AOL executive and current CEO of Monumental Sports and Entertainment—the Washington, D.C. sports conglomerate that owns the city's NHL, NBA, WNBA, NBA G-League, and AFL teams—is a perfect example of a sports owner who uses strategic partnerships with startups to improve his teams' in-game performance. In particular, Leonsis signed a multi-year partnership deal with STRIVR— Sports Training in Virtual Reality—following a disappointing 2014-15 season for the Washington Capitals. With the partnership, Leonsis was the first sports owner to bring virtual reality training to an NBA, NHL, and WNBA team.

Sports organizations, like all businesses, must innovate to meet the increasing expectations from their fans. But not every sports team innovates the same way. A sports team's approach to innovation is a result of the team's ownership style; teams owned by investment firms or groups of individuals with investment backgrounds are more likely to establish accelerator programs to support investments in several startups, while those owned by a majority owner opt for innovative practices that require less capital and time commitments, such as partnerships.

CHAPTER 3

THE VALUE OF AN ACCELERATOR

———

"Successful innovation is not a single breakthrough. It is not a sprint. It is not an event for the solo runner. Successful innovation is a team sport; it's a relay race."

—NGUYEN QUYEN

Running a startup is much like rebuilding a sports team: You need to lose in order to start winning.

Losing can be a valuable learning experiences for both athletes and entrepreneurs. For sports teams, the process of tanking has grown in popularity among bottom-dwelling teams, with the idea that losing on purpose would provide them better positioning in the draft, which leads to selecting more talented young athletes to build a team around. For startups, it takes about four years to reach positive annual cash flows.

"Trust the process" became the Philadelphia 76ers fan base's mantra while former 76ers General Manager Sam Hinkie fielded a purposefully unsuccessful team prior to the 2013-14 season. The idea was to undergo several seasons of poor performance to stockpile draft picks and eventually build a winning team in the future. Over a four-season stretch, the 76ers lost a total of 253 games, winning only one out of every five games. While 76ers were understandably angry at their organization at the time, they eventually came to embrace it, even raising a banner of Hinkie, who resigned as GM during the 2016 season, to honor him at the 76ers' 2017 NBA Draft Fan Party. For the 2017-18 season, "the process" showed its potential, as the 76ers qualified for the playoffs for the first time since 2012.

Similarly, entrepreneurs need to fail in order to learn how to succeed, and accelerators exist to provide a safety net and learning curve. By developing accelerator programs, sports teams are able to not only invest in several different startups simultaneously but also work closely together to provide the resources needed for growth and a symbiotic relationship between the team and startups.

* * *

The Los Angeles Dodgers have a history full of firsts. Back when they were the Brooklyn Dodgers, they were the first MLB team to broadcast a game on television in 1939. The Dodgers were also the first MLB team to sign an African-American player, Jackie Robinson, in 1947. And, on April 15, 2015, they became the first professional sports team to launch an accelerator program aimed at technology startups in the sports and entertainment industry.

The Dodgers' attraction to entrepreneurs began in 2012 when Guggenheim Partners purchased the team for $2 billion. With only seven MLB teams owned by a firm or company rather than an individual, it is uncommon—but efficient— for a team to be owned by a group. For one, such ownership brings in a wealth of individuals to make decisions not only related to sports but also business. The Guggenheim Partners' purchase brought the entrepreneurial and investor spirit to Los Angeles, as Mark Walter, the chairman of the Dodgers, co-founded the firm in 2000.

Along with Walter, Guggenheim Partners recruited former NBA player Earvin "Magic" Johnson to join the bid for the baseball team. In addition to being an NBA Hall of Famer, Johnson had his fair share of experience in entrepreneurship, having established in 1987 Magic Johnson Enterprises, an investment conglomerate worth an estimated $1 billion. Magic Johnson Enterprises currently holds assets in industries ranging from sports technology to beauty products: Walker & Company, ShotTracker, and Mitu, to name a few.

Following the McCourts' disastrous management of the team, the new ownership group inherited the laughingstock of the MLB. Yet the change in ownership also marked a dramatic shift in the Dodgers' performance, as the team returned to the playoffs in 2013. Suddenly, the Dodgers' payroll was on the rise again, leapfrogging the New York Yankees in team payroll for the 2014 season with a total of $235 million owed to players.

In order to finance their lucrative contracts, the Dodgers turned to their two main leaders of the Dodgers ownership group: Johnson and Walter Isaacson. Both had a wealth of knowledge in the area of entrepreneurship, and, due to the success of both Johnson and Isaacson as investors, several startups started pitching to the group. That's when Tucker Kain, the chief financial officer of the Dodgers, had an idea.

"As we came in, and started looking at opportunities the Dodgers had in front of them, [the ownership group] saw many great, smart, innovative young companies approaching us. ... What we realized is that using a platform like the Dodgers to validate those products, and at the same time, solve some of our own problems, made a lot of sense," Kain said to SoCal Tech in an interview in 2015. "With the background of our ownership group, and their interest in putting capital to use and our resources to work, we saw the opportunity to create strategic partnerships. That not [only] include[s] the relationships and network that our owners bring to bear, but also capital."

Initially, Kain and his team set up the accelerator program to be a three-month residency, providing the young companies with a $120,000 investment, free office space, access to mentors such as Johnson and Walter, and the attachment of the Dodgers brand to the emerging startups. Prior to the launch, the Dodgers partnered with the international advertising agency R/GA to boost the services that they could provide to their investment projects. In exchange for these services, the Dodgers and R/GA hold a combined 6% stake in each of the startups. For the startups, perhaps the biggest benefit from the relationship is what that the young entrepreneurs can learn from the ownership group's partners.

"In a lot of ways, [the partners] all realize how early businesses are funded and started, and also understand the opportunity something like Dodger Stadium gives to pilot some of those opportunities," Kain explained. "All of that combined can change the odds of success for companies. There are lots of great, innovative young businesses, but lots of them fail, unfortunately. The question is: How do you differentiate those companies, and pick which ones will succeed?"

At the beginning, it was quite difficult for the program to determine which companies would be accepted into the inaugural class, because the accelerator saw nearly 600 applications following the launch, as reported by a press release. Yet Kain knew exactly what the partners wanted to see in a startup in order for them to invest in it; he made sure the company's goals aligned well with the Dodgers' plans of creating more value to the team's brand.

"We were looking for places where we could be strategic, and add value, making sure it wasn't a one way street. We want the Dodgers brand, and R/GA's core competencies to be very valuable and strategic to these companies," Kain said. "We also wanted to make sure the companies helped address some issues in our business. We definitely layered them over our own business and combined that with the ability for us to be strategic, where we could apply our mentor network, and make sure we found the ten most interesting and collaborative businesses to bring into the program."

Despite being a professional baseball team, the Dodgers were not necessarily looking for startups in the baseball world. The accelerator leadership team approached the selection process with a broader focus, looking for ways to improve upon the team's brand beyond what the Dodgers can deliver on-field. The program wanted companies that could add value to the fan experience and the sports industry as a whole rather than just how the companies could benefit their baseball club.

"It's not just about coming up with a better baseball bat or working with the Dodgers," Stephen Plumlee, managing director of R/GA Ventures, said in a press release. "Our definition of sports is much broader than just the major leagues; it touches on things like fan engagement and data analytics that really have a global application."

In a separate interview with GeekWire, Plumlee stressed the notion that the program looked for more mature startups who needed the additional assistance to manage their growth and development.

"Rather than a startup 101 pre-seed program, this is much more about later-stage companies about to hit the hockey stick of growth," Plumlee said.

The program announced the 10 startups that would be part of its first class Aug. 24, 2015, with a notable focus on the intersection of sports and technology. Companies accepted into the program included Swish Analytics, a daily fantasy sports lineup optimizer; ProDay, a mobile platform that allows its users to virtually work out with professional athletes; and

Appetize, a mobile point-of-sale application that allows for a more fan-friendly experience when making transactions at sports and entertainment venues, allowing fans to pay for transactions using newer forms of payment, such as Apply Pay and EMV.

For Appetize, the Dodgers Accelerator program was the next step for the young company to expand its operations nationwide. Prior to their acceptance, the startup provided services to Fenway Park in Boston and Citi Field in Flushings, New York. After a month in the accelerator, Appetize's software appeared in 32 Live Nations Venue, of which Dodgers Stadium is an affiliate. The rapid growth experienced by the startup can be attributed to the connections that Appetize co-founder and Chief Strategy Officer Kevin Anderson made through the Dodgers Accelerator, referring to the program as a "winning partnership." Anderson also credited Plumlee for assisting the company as it experienced its rapid growth.

"We are now poised to seize market leadership," Anderson said in a 2017 interview with Bankless Times. "In every venue Appetize launches, GMs see immediate revenue growth, a vastly improved guest ordering experience, massive cost savings and turnkey profit increase. That capability is driving our strong referral and aggressive momentum across the major venue concessions market."

* * *

As the Dodgers groomed startups into mature, successful companies, other professional sports teams took notice and began creating their own programs supporting entrepreneurs. In 2016, the Philadelphia 76ers announced the opening of the 76ers Innovation Lab, while the Minnesota Vikings also joined the startup bandwagon, announcing that their new stadium would include an accelerator for Minnesota-based tech startups.

After seeing the success of the company in the two years of existence, the Dodgers Accelerator rebranded itself to become the Global Sports Venture Studio on Jan. 8, 2018. Maintaining its partnership with R/GA, the program shifted to a more collaborative effort, viewing innovation as a team sport, as displayed on the top of the studio's website.

"This is really the next iteration of our sports tech engagement at the Dodgers," Kain said to LA Business Journal following the name change. "This new structure is going to allow for more of a rolling schedule and a deeper, more dynamic and more nimble level of engagement with startups instead of being constricted by a calendar."

With the new approach, the studio hopes to provide a more hands-on experience to its companies, ditching the three-month accelerator format and committing to work with the company for an extended period. Additionally, the updated model has a dedicated full-time staff of 10 employees, double the number from the original accelerator program, and also increased access to R/GA creative resources. With offices currently operating in New York City and Los Angeles, the studio hopes to expand globally with an office in London within the year.

"Our programs are designed to provide value to our corporate program partners and to startups," Plumlee said. "By evolving the program model towards a more collaborative and global approach, the Global Sports Venture Studio will better enable program partners to capitalize on disruptive technologies and emerging consumer behaviors on an ongoing basis."

By providing financing and consulting, the Dodgers Accelerator made sure its startups had the tools and knowledge necessary to succeed and grow while also finding ways to incorporate the disruptive technology into the Dodgers experience. Under the direction of seasoned entrepreneurs, founders like Kevin Anderson immediately saw the value of working in an accelerator program that benefited not only his company but also the Dodgers.

* * *

By 2016, "the process" was still ongoing in Philadelphia. The 76ers' struggles continued with the team dropping 54 games that season, yet a silver lining emerged: The 76ers owned the first overall pick in that summer's draft.

But while the Sixers were looking to improve their on-court performance, they also made an announcement that would benefit them financially. On April 12, 2016, 76ers CEO Scott O'Neill announced the plan to launch the Sixers Innovation Lab Crafted by Kimball. Located in the 76ers practice facility in Camden, New Jersey, the Sixers Innovation Lab works with early-stage startup companies across multiple sectors— including sports technology and pet care—to increase the value of both the startups and the 76ers as an organization.

"As the Philadelphia 76ers organization eagerly awaits our move into a state-of-the-art basketball training complex, we thought it provided the perfect opportunity to include the Sixers Innovation Lab Crafted by Kimball, to drive the entrepreneurial spirit that is at the very foundation of this region," O'Neill said in a press release. "We are fortunate to have assembled an unmatched roster of partners that have deep and seemingly unending material relationships in sports, media, technology and consumer-facing businesses that will serve the early stage companies housed under our roof and provide every advantage to help these aspiring leaders fulfill their dreams."

When looking for an individual to help run the lab, O'Neill turned to an old colleague and friend who had seasoned experienced with entrepreneurship. O'Neill found his guy in Seth Berger, former CEO and founder of AND 1, a popular basketball apparel brand in the 1990s and 2000s. For Berger, the decision to become the managing director of the Sixers Innovation Lab was an easy one.

"I love working with startups and early stage entrepreneurs, and I really like being a part of Scott's team," Berger explained in a phone interview with me.

With a successful entrepreneur running the lab, the Sixers Innovation Lab was ready to start accepting startups. Differing from the Dodgers Accelerator's approach to accepting startups, Berger stressed the importance of prioritizing the team behind the startup idea rather than focusing on accepting startups in the sports world.

"First and foremost, we look for a managing team that we like, a person or people that we really believe in," Berger explained. "Second, an idea that we think is unique and has a potential to be a really good business. Doesn't have to be great right away, and part of our job is to help mold good ideas into great businesses. Also finding businesses that we feel like we can add unique value to, otherwise we become any other investor or check writer."

While the first startup to be accepted into the Sixers Innovation Lab, Monster Roster, is related to sports, the other three companies working within the accelerator have little or no relation to sports: They include Live Life Nice, a digital media company that spreads messages on social media to inspire others to be nice in the world; U GIT GUD, an online tutoring tool aimed to help train eSports players; and Doc & Phoebe'9s Cat Company, a cat-food dispensary tool that focuses on the prevention of overfeeding pet cats.

Despite all four of the companies serving drastically different markets, Berger identified how all of them work toward a common goal.

"I think every business that exists, that survives, is trying to solve a problem. Each of these businesses are trying to figure out what problem are these businesses trying to solve and secondarily, who's the end user and how well can we know the end user. If you think about in those standpoints, what problem are we trying to solve and for whom are we trying to solve it, from then you are just trying to get your business plan to be a straight line from point A to point B," Berger said.

To further illustrate this point, Berger compared Elder's Monster Roster to Doc & Phoebe's Cat Company.

"So, Dylan's, for example, is trying to solve a problem for people who are in the Daily Fantasy space and losing too much money. And then you want to find out about your end user, is that a 28-year-old, 34 year-old, 22-year-old male? Is it male or female? Where does that person live? How much does that person bet on daily fantasy? All of those sorts of things."

"It's the same thing for Doc & Phoebe. Doc & Phoebe is trying to solve for euthanasia being the number one cause of death for cats in America because cats are overfed. ... The problem we are trying to solve is the cat's stomach is the size of a ping pong ball, and we're serving it as if it has the stomach of a small human being. And your customer is the cat parent—how do you make this product easy to understand, easy to buy, and easy to use? So, those are really the same kind of problems that you are trying to solve for Monster Roster as you are for Doc & Phoebe."

The Sixers Innovation Lab's dedication to serving early-stage companies, unlike the Dodgers Accelerator, which focuses on mature companies, leads to a more hands-on approach to the startups' growth and development strategy. Upon being accepted, three of the four accepted companies, including Monster Roster and Doc & Phoebe's, underwent major rebranding through the discretion of the program, demonstrating the Innovation team's understanding of emerging startups. If these companies did not rebrand then, it would be too difficult to change in the future.

Originally named the NoBowl Feeding System, Doc & Phoebe's Cat Company started as a Kickstarter campaign in early 2016. The startup exceeded its goal of $36,000 in just four days and ended up receiving a total amount of $250,000 in crowdfunding. Upon its acceptance into the 76ers Innovation Lab, Berger and the rest of the team suggested changing the name to better represent what the company provided to their customers. By incorporating the word "cat" into its brand name, the company clearly signaled to pet owners who the product was designed for.

"Under the new name Doc & Phoebe's, the brand and packaging will aim to target consumers and cat owners," Doc & Phoebe's CEO Dr. Liz Bales said in an interview with Pet Age. "We are very excited to share the future of cat care and our rebrand with all pet parents in order to make cats happier and healthier than ever."

Monster Roster dealt with the same issue. Originally named And1 Analytics—coincidentally an ode to Berger's sports apparel brand—Elder's company lacked an engaging name that captured consumer's attention while also informing them of the brand's offering. And while And1 Analytics was not failing at the time, it was not bringing in enough revenue as Elder struggled to develop an effective monetization strategy due to his lack of business experience. In addition to expanding Andı Analytics' revenue streams by integrating baseball into its algorithm, which at the time only produced NBA and NFL lineups, Berger also initiated a rebranding strategy.

"For every company and every brand, you want to minimize the amount of dollars you want to spend to grow your brand, so you want to come up with a name that is immediately meaningful to your end user. So Andı Analytics isn't in any way meaningful to a customer. Monster Roster immediately says what the business is about," Berger said.

Another major factor that separates the Sixers Innovation Lab from the Dodgers Accelerator is the willingness to allow the companies to work in the Innovation Lab for as long as needed. Unlike the three-month Dodgers program, the Sixers Innovation Lab does not have a time constraint on its startups and is committed to providing the necessary tools in order to prepare the company for either an exit strategy or to file for an initial public offering.

"It's early; we've been at it for a year and a half now, and these are all five-year outcomes," Berger explained. "It's early for exits, but we are pretty optimistic. But there is no time pressure to do anything quickly."

While the Los Angeles Dodgers were the first professional sports team to create an accelerator program, the Philadelphia 76ers were able to adapt that model into their own accelerator. The more hands-on approach coupled with the elimination of any time constraints has allowed the Sixers Innovation team, along with the startups' founders, to turn their good idea into a great business. And, despite the 76ers finally making the playoffs, the process for the Innovation Lab never ends.

* * *

Corporate innovation does not occur overnight. It cannot be implemented by a single individual. While it is true that a certain entrepreneurial mindset should be promoted throughout a company, a shift in company culture could be costly, not only in terms of time but also in human capital.

By examining professional sports teams' approach to accelerator programs, companies in other industries can learn how to efficiently manage multiple startups at once. Accelerators provide firms with an efficient way to involve themselves with emerging startups who can then return the investment made by the company through continuous innovation.

Potentially the most important step in building a corporate accelerator, or incubator, program is to select the individual who will be in charge of managing not only the accelerator's team but also the startups' teams. The 76ers set a good example of what type of person should be given this responsibility through the selection of Berger as managing director. As founder of AND1, Berger has a wealth of experience in the entrepreneurial world and knows how to manage other entrepreneurs.

Furthermore, having these experienced entrepreneurs making the strategic decisions for the accelerator makes selecting startups to work with more efficient, especially when you receive over 500 applications; they have a solid idea of not only what ideas have potential but also the traits of the startup's founder and if they fit the bill. While many may think it's best to prioritize the idea in front of the person, keep in mind that the partnership will be only as good as the relationship between the main parties involved. When investing in startups, make sure that the individual running the startup is coachable.

It is equally as important for both the investor and the benefactor to understand that the partnership is a two-way street. A disparity in benefits for the two parties can cause tension to rise and working as a team to become more difficult. It is essential as an investor to recognize that your main priority is providing the necessary resources for your startup to succeed. On the flip side, an entrepreneur should not take this investment for granted, but take advantage of the resources provided to build value not only for both the brand itself and the investor.

For a startup to be successful under an accelerator program, the founder must be willing to learn and work in partnership with the management team to ensure that both parties receive benefits.

CHAPTER 4

THE COLLEGE DROPOUT

—

"It's not about ideas. It's about making ideas happen."

—SCOTT BELSKY

"It's now or never."

After dropping out of school not once but *twice*, Elder faced yet another tough decision to make on the future of his education and business.

Finals were just a week away, but Elder had more important things on his mind.

With the legalization of sports betting on the horizon, Elder wanted to resume his position as CEO of Monster Roster, but a few months before that he decided to return to George-town University and continue his studies for the spring 2018 semester.

"It's now or never."

Elder of course could have waited for the finalization of the U.S. Supreme Court's decision and returned to Monster Roster over the summer, but that would have been too late. He knew that he needed to be there full time, as soon as possible, to start prepping his company for this huge opportunity.

"It's now or never."

Elder went with his gut, leaving Georgetown for the second time in two years. Leaving Georgetown two weeks before finals started. Leaving Georgetown to rejoin his colleagues at the Sixers Innovation Lab to continue his pursuit as an entrepreneur.

Because Elder trusted them.

* * *

The top 1% of daily fantasy sports players win 90% of the money.

That is the inspiration behind Monster Roster, a daily fantasy sports lineup recommender co-founded by Elder, a "current sophomore" at Georgetown University.

"When I first started playing DFS I deposited $100, lost it right away, deposited another $100, and lost it right away too because I was making lineups as an average sports fan," Elder said.

To combat this issue, he and his friend developed an algorithm in high school to predict individual athletes' performances for NBA and NFL games and created lineups that would win. After sharing some of their winning lineups on social media, the duo decided to start selling the lineups for profit.

While his friend dropped out of the business before leaving for college, Elder continued to work on his company, originally called And1 Analytics, throughout his freshman year at Georgetown. Elder quickly realized, however, that he needed more assistance to make his company grow.

"We had a revenue and a product that worked, so I knew there was a market for this," Elder said. "I had never run a business before and I needed external help to take the business to where I wanted to take it."

In spring 2016, one of Elder's friends—who happened to be a 76ers fan—showed him the team's plan to start an accelerator program; Elder decided to apply while procrastinating homework. During the summer, Elder heard back from the Sixers Innovation Lab and received an invitation to present his business to Managing Director Seth Berger and Director of Operations Rhyan Truett, but Elder found preparing for the meeting difficult as he had no previous business experience.

"I set up a whole business plan for them, and they ripped it apart," Elder said of his initial presentation. "So I did it again, and it was a little better the second time, and they invited me in the beginning of August to pitch to the board of governors. I put together a whole deck to pitch to them and after the presentation I kind of knew what would happen because me and Seth just sat down for four hours to talk about the future of the business."

Elder's gut reaction following his presentation to the board was correct: Andi Analytics became the first company accepted into the Sixers Innovation Lab. But before Elder could agree to join the team in Philadelphia, he had to face what he called the toughest decision he has made to this point. By agreeing to work on his company full time under the Sixers Innovation Lab, Elder had to put his Georgetown education on hold after one year, which led to a consequential discussion with his parents.

"It wasn't something where I was just, 'Hey, Mom and Dad, I want to do this'; it was a group discussion," Elder said. "I never thought of myself as someone who'd be a 'college dropout,' and I knew I wasn't going to be the next Mark Zuckerberg, but I have the best parents in the world who supported me, and, as we continued to talk it through, it became clear to me that this is what I want to do, and I am passionate about it," Elder said.

* * *

Before Elder had his discussion with his parents, he had to have an internal discussion with himself to determine if he trusted the Sixers Innovation Lab as a viable plan for him and his business. Taking a year off from school was a huge risk for Elder, and he realized the importance of placing his trust with the right people in succeeding as a business.

So, what made Elder—a kid fresh off his first year at college who had never taken a business class—trust Berger and the rest of the team?

Well, in his mind, the trust was forced. Not in the sense that Berger aggressively pressured Elder into accepting his invitation to the Sixers Innovation Lab, but more so due to Elder's awareness of his own skills and expertise: He knew that he needed to work with seasoned entrepreneurs to make his idea into a successful business.

"Coming in, I did not know how to run a business at all. I kind of had to dive headfirst into it and had no choice but to trust them," Elder recalled. "But, clearly, with Seth's experience and being part of a larger organization that were making a lot of strides in terms of business opportunities, the owners are very New Age in their thinking and that definitely brought a lot of trust at the beginning, and that trust built over time given the success we were seeing."

David Williams, a serial entrepreneur and author of *The 7 Non Negotiables of Winning*, highlights trust as a necessary pillar for business success. Williams suggests that one method to build trust within organizations is to "never judge—seek first to understand."

After getting his first presentation ripped apart by Berger and Truett, Elder could have retreated. He could have been discouraged and given up on his dream. However, Elder did not judge Berger and Truett for their feedback, instead choosing to view it as constructive criticism—as an opportunity to better hone in on his vision for his company.

On the flip side, the Sixers Innovation Lab did not judge Elder on his poor first presentation. The team knew that Elder came into the pitch with little to no help on the business side and understood this was his first time pitching his idea as a business to potential investors. By understanding each other, Elder, Berger, and the rest of the Innovation team built a solid foundation of trust.

"The fact that he trusted me was all I needed to see. To bring a 19-year-old kid, with admittedly no business experience, in as the first company into the innovation lab, made it easy for me to reciprocate that level of trust," Elder added.

* * *

Elder suffered a quick scare about a week before he was about to start at the Sixers Innovation Lab. On Aug. 11, 2016, Draft-Kings announced that the daily fantasy sports website would ban lineup selling, which was how And1 Analytics operated.

"Because they did this right before I was going to the lab, I was like 'Shit, this is going to screw up my chance here,'" Elder said. But with the help of the experienced entrepreneur in Berger, Elder was able to work with the rest of the Sixers Innovation Lab to change the business model and transition it from a lineup selling service to a lineup optimizer, allowing users to construct their own lineups based on the app's suggestions. Elder spent the first couple of weeks re-evaluating the business strategy, even going as far as to implement a rebranding strategy.

"One of the first days there, I'm in a meeting with Seth and the creative team just talking about why I started the company, and they took that information and gave me 20 different options for company names and logos," Elder said. "Having that bridge to experts in the creative stuff was super helpful, especially because I'm not good with that."

This example leads into another one of William's tips for building trust: "help others with critical tasks."

Knowing that Elder had little business knowledge, Berger recognized his duty to help Elder overcome this unforeseen challenge. Rebranding can be daunting for a CEO, especially one new to the business environment, but due to Berger's commitment to the brand's success, Elder knew it was the right decision.

So, on that August day, And1 Analytics rebranded into Monster Roster, coupled with new colors and a logo. With the help from the creative team, Elder was able to implement a drastic change to his company despite not having expertise or any experience in that aspect of business.

Elder placed the future of And1 Analytics in the hands of the Sixers Innovation Lab. Due to his lack of knowledge in the business world, Elder had to fully trust Berger and the rest of the team during the rebranding process, by recognizing that these changes are in the best interest of the company.

From the Sixers standpoint, they admittedly took a gamble investing in a company run by someone who could not pass high school calculus. Yet they found something even more valuable in the young entrepreneur: a great idea and willingness to learn. By identifying the opportunity presented by the Sixers Innovation Lab and deciding to work full time on his company rather than returning to school, Elder demonstrated his passion and commitment to his startup. Elder took full advantage of the benefits and used the resources given to him to improve his business, proving to the Sixers that they made the right decision.

* * *

In accepting his invitation to the Sixers Innovation Lab, Elder knew the opportunity would legitimize his business, especially when meeting key business individuals.

In the business world, connections are everything.

Connections can lead to a new investment, a new job, and even a new business idea.

And, in the case of Monster Roster and its work under the Sixers Innovation Lab, Elder had to build these relationships through connections on a foundation of trust. Trust in the Innovation Lab to put him in front of individuals who could help the business succeed and, more importantly, trust among Elder and whichever connection he decides to take advice from. Luckily, the connections that were associated with the management team helped Elder overcome yet another set of challenges that he faced.

"I had zero business experience at first but knew more about daily fantasy sports as a product than anyone else there," Elder said. "Conveying my message and ideas to them and then combining their business expertise and making both paths fit, because some great ideas for daily fantasy sports that I had wouldn't allow us to scale as a company. So working through things I didn't know with things they didn't know to create a new business was quite challenging."

Elder struggled to align daily fantasy sports users' needs with a business's needs. However, a simple meeting organized by Berger granted Elder the opportunity to talk with one of the leading experts in daily fantasy sports.

DraftKings, one of the largest daily fantasy sports contest providers, just so happened to be a sponsor of the Sixers Innovation Lab. Because DraftKings users are Monster Roster's target market, Berger thought it would be a good idea to set up and introduce DraftKings CEO Jason Robbins to Elder. On Sept. 14, 2016, Elder and Berger flew up to Boston to discuss Monster Roster with Robbins and build a relationship with the company.

At the time of the meeting, Monster Roster was still in the midst of its redevelopment stage following DraftKings' ban on lineup selling. The app had not been launched yet, and Elder viewed this meeting as an opportunity to pick Robbins' brain and get advice on his product.

"We weren't pitching to Jason Robbins to buy this business, it was more like 'Hey, can we get some advice on how to make this product work?' and stuff that we didn't know about because he's been in the daily fantasy sports industry for a decade," Elder said.

The meeting proved beneficial for Elder and for the growth of Monster Roster. Since being introduced to Robbins, Monster Roster and DraftKings have had affiliate partnerships, such as offering a free week trial for Monster Roster when creating a DraftKings account, which drove new users to both companies. However, the key takeaway from the meeting had nothing to do with partnerships, but rather the app's user experience.

Robbins pointed out a major flaw in Monster Roster's user experience. Initially, Monster Roster's app layout required users to go though several different screens to craft their lineups. Robbins saw this setup as a negative.

"During that meeting Jason said, 'People don't want to do a lot of clicks; they just want to do one click,' so a simple change we made was to have one click to select a player and move on to the next position," Elder explained.

Robbins understood the behaviors of DraftKings' consumers. Considering that all daily fantasy sports contests have hard deadlines to register (usually before the first game of the night starts), users want to be able to generate their lineups with Monster Roster as quickly as possible. By getting rid of the two click process, Elder successfully sped up the rate at which a user can select a lineup, providing them with more time to input the lineup into a contest.

Elder admitted that he would not have thought of that change on his own and owes credit to Berger for organizing the meeting with Robbins.

"Three weeks into working with the Sixers, I got a meeting with the CEO of DraftKings, while three months ago I was playing drinking games at Georgetown. I never would have got that meeting by myself," Elder reflected.

But as Elder spent more time in the entrepreneurial environment, he became more comfortable working in a business setting, knowing that he could trust Berger to provide assistance when necessary. At the same time, Berger's trust in Elder expanded as he gained more business experience. While Berger advised Elder throughout the rebranding process, he also understood that Monster Roster was Elder's company and therefore allowed Elder to implement his own vision for the startup.

"One of the best parts about Seth and the Sixers Innovation team is that I have 100% creative freedom to make changes and improvements to anything that I think will benefit the company," Elder said.

Elder identified product development as his main area of focus as CEO, which includes designing the site, adding new features (such as prop bets), and ensuring that the user experience within the app and site is as easy as possible. Product development is the foundation of Monster Roster, and it is up to Elder to determine the best methods for developing his product to appeal to Monster Roster's target market. Luckily for Elder, he aligned perfectly with the ideal Monster Roster consumer: a college-aged male sports fan.

"Thinking about it from a user perspective, I think I have a little bit of an advantage there because I am the target user, and I get to build the product too, so anything I want to see in the product, we can make happen," Elder said. "And not what I want to see as a CEO, but what I want to see as a user."

* * *

The tricky part of investing in companies run by college students is the uncertainty of their level of commitment to the company. Being a college student is hard enough, balancing your social life with your studies. However, that balance becomes even more difficult when you are a CEO as a college student.

Elder faced the difficult decision of whether to pursue his college education or continue to work on his company and put his education on hold. However, in Elder's case, he had to make this tough decision twice.

"When I made the decision to take a year off of school back in June 2016, and at the same time I decided, along with my family, that I would do the best job I can so that it would be the hardest decision to come back to school. Because that would've meant I did a great job," Elder said.

To the delight of the young CEO, Elder did just that. With the help of the team at the Sixers Innovation Lab, Elder grew Monster Roster into a successful business. After raising more money during the spring of 2016, Elder once again had to face the tough decision of following his passion project or returning to school. Elder ultimately decided to forgo yet another semester of college, noting that he had to be part of the team following the new funding.

After taking three semesters off from Georgetown, Elder began to feel lonely and disconnected from his friends back at school.

"I wanted a real college experience, I wanted to have real friends," Elder explained when asked why he wanted to return to Georgetown. "In Philly, I had an amazing time, and Mondays through Fridays were great, because I got to work on something I loved every single day, but on the weekends it got kind of bland after a while. If I were to have taken any-more time off, I would've felt disconnected from my friends in terms of my experience versus their experiences, even if I visited on the weekends. I honestly did not come back to get a degree; I came back for the college experience, and everyone who supports me in life understands."

Elder's internal conflict about working on his company versus being back at school highlights another aspect of why professional sports accelerators help entrepreneurs excel. Berger understood Elder's desire to return to Georgetown and provided Elder with resources and advice to make the decision easier for him, such as helping him hire a replacement CEO in Elder's absence. But even that made Elder a little uneasy at first.

"When we were hiring the new CEO, one of my reservations was what if this new CEO comes in, does the best job he can, but for some reason out of his control the company doesn't work, like if sports gambling doesn't become legal or DFS becomes illegal," Elder noted. "He's getting paid a salary to do the job that I was doing, and runs the company for two years. Well, then this guy would've made 400k, and I would've made no money. It's not that it's not fair, because life's not fair, but it's more of a question I had. Seth's point was that I was right, but in terms of post-Monster Roster life, the way to think about it is more I've enjoyed not having to answer to anyone and having so much freedom, how to build a business."

The realization that Elder's experience with Monster Roster was about more than just money—it was also all the learning involved with it—made the founder more comfortable with the idea of leaving the company in someone else's hands. The next step required finding that perfect someone, so during the fall of 2017, Berger and the rest of the Sixers Innovation Lab helped Elder find the ideal candidate.

"In terms of picking a new CEO, it was pretty easy," Elder admitted. "The new CEO, Kevin Lee, worked with Seth at And1 and has run a couple of his own companies since then. The process was basically Seth knew I wanted to go back to school, reached out to him and a couple of other people, I interviewed them all, and I felt Kevin was the best option. Seth made it very easy because of his connections. I would have no way to reach out to Kevin without Seth."

Similarly to how Berger's connections led to Monster Roster adapting a different business strategy and user experience, the Sixers Innovation Lab provided Elder the necessary resources to adapt to his own personal desires. By hiring someone who Berger had previously worked with, Elder felt confident and comfortable with his decision to step away from his role as CEO of Monster Roster and return to his friends back at school.

The Sixers Innovation Lab placed a high level of trust in Elder's commitment to the company. While those at the lab was willing to let him return for the semester, they still had high expectations for his involvement with company decisions. When Elder returned to Georgetown for the 2018 spring semester, he continued to be involved with Monster Roster outside of a CEO role. Elder held the position of chairman of Monster Roster, maintained his majority stake in the company, and returned to the Philadelphia office every so often for important meetings while he was a student. In fact, on the day classes resumed following spring break, Elder attended his first two classes, got on a train to Philadelphia, and attended a meeting with Berger and Lee. If that isn't commitment to your company, I don't know what is.

* * *

In today's NBA, the word "loyalty" carries a lot of weight.

NBA fans and teams have grown to appreciate those players who stick with a team through their entire careers after witnessing LeBron James leave Cleveland on two separate occasions and Kevin Durant joining the Golden State Warriors dynasty.

Loyalty is equally as important in the business world. Author David Williams describes a healthy organization as having individuals "who are loyal to each other. They keep their word and honor their journey."

So when the date of the U.S. Supreme Court ruling on the legality of sports betting came closer, and the outcome became clearer, Elder knew he needed to be a part of this journey. But he did not want to be on the sidelines watching; he wanted to be back in the driver's seat.

"It was a now-or-never thing for me to build this product up to get in a position where we either sell the business or have a lot of success as a cash flow-positive business. There was no waiting for me. I absolutely had a choice, but it didn't feel like a choice because it was like 'OK, I've invested so much into this; I see the potential in this, and it's now or never to make this happen.'"

Berger could have easily dismissed his advances, especially since they just hired a new CEO to take over duties while Elder returned to school. Yet Berger remained loyal to Elder, understanding that Monster Roster was Elder's company to run and take in whatever direction he envisioned.

The U.S. Supreme Court delivered its ruling on May 14, 2018. As expected, the ruling legalized sports betting, allowing states to pass their own legislation regarding sports betting, much to Elder's joy.

"We've completely pivoted our business to not only offer daily fantasy lineups, but also offer betting stuff," Elder explained. "It's been a huge boom from a success standpoint from us. We've been working since January testing our algorithm to make it work for sports-betting lines, such as player prop bets and game bets."

Monster Roster needed Elder there for these drastic changes. Not only because he had the most knowledge of daily fantasy sports and sports betting in general, but also because he represented Monster Roster's target user.

* * *

With Monster Roster, we see the inside workings of a young CEO and the business relationships that he has made along the way to run a successful business.

The success of Monster Roster is owed to the high level of trust that both parties invested in each other from the onset. Elder trusted Berger's business recommendations on the basis that he had a lot more knowledge in the field, mainly due to his experience running AND1, and Berger trusted Elder as a hard-working individual willing to learn.

Elder acknowledged that the Sixers Innovation Lab would be full of business experts and recognized that they were there to help, especially following his initial pitch to them.

For Berger, it was about placing trust not into the idea, but rather in the person behind the idea. Berger identified Elder early on as a hard-working individual who cared deeply about his idea, evident in Elder's willingness to reconstruct his pitch presentation based on his feedback.

Berger's hands-on approach to Monster Roster augmented Elder's trust in him, demonstrating to the young CEO that these individuals care about his company, and will do whatever is in their power to make it as successful as possible.

The business relationship between Berger and Elder was built on a foundation of trust, and the level of trust among the two individuals only increased over time, resulting in more creative freedom as a CEO for Elder. Because of that, Monster Roster is in a prime place for success, as it is projected to be cash flow positive by the end of the 2018 year—just two and a half years after being accepted into the accelerator—for the first time in the company's short existence.

CHAPTER 5

INNOVATION: A CAPITAL ADVANTAGE

---

*"You do not merely want to be considered the best of the best.
You want to be considered the only ones that do what you do."*

—JERRY GARCIA

On Sept. 15, 2017, the Washington Capitals opened training
camp for the upcoming season. Following the first practice,
Capitals captain Alex Ovechkin walked up to the podium
surrounded by reporters to give his first press conference
of the season. Coming off another early playoff departure
caused by the Pittsburgh Penguins, reporters were curious
about the captain's expectations for the team this season.

"We're not gonna be suck this year," Ovechkin stated in broken English.

As the captain, Ovechkin serves as the de facto spokesperson for the team. With a slight grin on his face, Ovechkin delivered the unofficial mantra for the Capitals' upcoming season. However, being a vocal leader is one thing, but leading by example is more effective for inspiring your teammates.

Ovechkin opened the season scoring back-to-back hat tricks in the first two games of the season, becoming the first NHL player to do so since 1917. If his teammates were not all-in on his claim prior to the season, they certainly were following his impressive individual efforts. These efforts, combined with his confidence, trickled down to the other Capitals players throughout the season, continuing through the playoffs, when the team proved to the world that it was "not gonna be suck this year" as the players captured the first Stanley Cup in franchise history on June 7, 2018.

Similar to hockey, innovation is a team sport that requires strong leadership by example. Individuals in a corporation must be aware of the firm's goals and objectives while also sharing an understanding as to why innovation is important. Those who do not buy into the approach stifle creativity and slow down innovation.

That's why Ted Leonsis exemplifies what it means to be an innovative business leader. As CEO of Monumental Sports & Entertainment, Leonsis controls the ownership group's vision. Because of his affinity for technology, Leonsis stresses the importance of innovation in all aspects of his business— from fan engagement to in-game performances—and serves as an example for the rest of his employees by embracing these new technologies.

Leonsis' willingness to embrace innovation extends not only to the rest of the Monumental front office but also down to the players and coaches, setting Monumental Sports up for success both on and off the ice through strategic partnerships with emerging startups and brands.

* * *

Leonsis' attraction to technology began during his days at Georgetown University when he decided to write his senior thesis on Ernest Hemingway's *The Old Man and the Sea*. Trying to prove that parts of the book were written prior to its 1950 publication date, Leonsis decided to seek help from technology and produced a computer program to obtain information on literature. The computer program supported Leonsis' hypothesis, but more importantly, it demonstrated to Leonsis the power of technology.

Soon after college, Leonsis launched his first venture, LIST, a technology magazine focusing on the personal computer industry, after looking at a TV guide in a grocery store and wondering why there wasn't one of these for computers. Upon selling LIST for $40 million after two years, Leonsis started his second business, Redgate Communications Corporation, which was quickly acquired by AOL, where Leonsis climbed the corporate ladder, eventually serving as the vice chairman.

While much of Leonsis' success can be attributed to his work ethic, his belief in innovation and embracing technological advances allowed him to be a successful entrepreneur, which he has now translated to his sports teams.

After making his fortune during the tech boom as an AOL senior executive, Leonsis learned to appreciate the opportunities presented by new technologies in all aspects of life, even professional sports. But to fully understand the impact of Leonsis' innovative thinking, compare it to other sports owners who value the "old school" aspect of sports and avoid new technologies, which is highlighted by Derek Belch's experience as a CEO.

* * *

The world of professional sports is filled with traditionalists—people who do not like change. Whether it's an NFL rule moving up kickoffs to the 35-yard line or the MLB introducing video replays to make up for human error, there will always be some pushback from athletes, coaches, or even owners. The introduction of MLB video reviews in 2013 received mixed reviews from players and coaches, with former MLB player Josh Hamilton famously saying: "C'mon MLB, that's terrible, and you can quote me on that," after a replay review went against him. Yet some coaches and players embrace change and value the potential added benefits of innovation, and Derek Belch took full advantage of that.

A former kicker for the Stanford University football team, Belch was brought on to be a graduate assistant coach for the team he'd once played for while also pursuing a master's degree in media studies/virtual reality in 2013. It was during his work alongside professor Jeremy Bailenson, a world-renowned virtual reality expert, that an idea was hatched. Virtual reality piqued Belch's interest after he took Bailenson's class as an undergrad and knew he wanted to work alongside Bailenson for his thesis that concentrated on the integration of virtual reality with football.

Working together in Stanford's virtual reality lab, Belch and Bailenson came up with a virtual reality experience designed to help the quarterback make quicker decisions. By filming practices with multiple cameras, Belch and Bailenson edited the footage and adapted it to a virtual environment and uploaded it to a VR headset.

Whoever put on the headset immediately filled the quarterback's shoes, giving them the ability to read defensive coverage, recognize blitzes, and identify open receivers without stepping onto a field. Belch and Bailenson spent much of 2014 sharpening their technology while working closely with the Stanford football team.

"When I was doing my master's thesis while coaching at Stanford, I was fully intending on going down the path of giving coaching a shot," Belch said. "The academic thesis was so successful, and the potential of the product had so much promise that I sat down long and hard, but it was a no-brainer that if I don't give this a shot, when am I ever going to give running a business a shot? I knew I always wanted to start my own company [but] didn't know what it was going to be [or] where it was going to be, so this was kind of the perfect storm for this opportunity and decided to give it a run."

With the realization that the product developed for his thesis held value, Belch couldn't pass up the opportunity to make an impact with professional athletes. In February 2015, Belch was flying out to Indianapolis to pitch STRIVR—Sports Training in Virtual Reality—to NFL coaches at the NFL Scouting Combine, hoping to get an in with an NFL team.

Through a demonstration to 10 coaches—and one hall-of-fame quarterback turned general manager—Belch showed the potential of the technology, encouraging all of them to put the headset on and give it a try.

"I was expecting something kinda cheesy, like video-game quality, and right when I was about to write them off, they put the headset on you and shoot, it's real," one NFL quarterback coach said of the meeting.

However, there were no immediate bites from NFL teams to partner with STRIVR. Perhaps it was the coaches' distaste of innovation, fearing that it would disrupt their veteran quarterback routine.

"Sports is very old school," Belch said when asked about the challenges STRIVR faced early on. "Very routine-oriented. Now throw in some cutting-edge technology that people must wrap their head around; it's not that easy."

But Belch was not worried. He knew he had a good product; he knew a market existed—he just needed more push. And that push arrived in the form of a Fox Sports article written by Bruce Feldman on March 11, 2015, which lead to STRIVR's first NFL client, the Dallas Cowboys.

"There was no more need to find a way in; a bunch of teams just started calling us," Belch recalled regarding the article. "Dallas was one of those teams. One of their assistants actually called Stanford because they didn't have my number and asked 'Hey, is there any way to get into contact with this Derek guy? [Head Coach] Jason Garrett would like to talk to him.' I was out there a few weeks later, and they were on board."

Belch decided to keep the partnership with the Cowboys under wraps, spending a great deal of time at their practice facility, where they were building a designated virtual reality room. STRIVR was also working on further developing their technology so it could be used for positions other than quarterback. But if Belch knew what would happen after word got out that the Cowboys were on board, he would have gone public with it earlier.

"News went public on ESPN.com that the Cowboys were working with us the first week of June, and that's what blew the lid off of it. We heard from 15 NFL teams in 12 hours after that," Belch said. "That was our coming-out party."

By the start of NFL training camp in late July 2015, three additional teams signed deals with STRIVR: the San Francisco 49ers, Minnesota Vikings, and Arizona Cardinals. Why just three out of the 15 that called? Well, that can be attributed to the stubbornness of some NFL team executives on their willingness to pay.

"Sports is an extremely challenging environment to operate in," Belch explained. "On the one hand, dollars are massive; on the other hand, the line of demarcation between player contracts and everything else is really thick, and they don't spend money on anything else besides player contracts. The willingness to pay and the 'Hey, we're the Dallas Cowboys; we're the Cleveland Cavaliers, give it to us for free and we will promote it for you.' That is really real and pretty much the mindset that teams have. Even the crappy teams believe that we should be happy to work with them; that happens all the time."

As of spring 2018, STRIVR has deals with 11 professional sports teams across the four major U.S. sports leagues and has ventured out into the retail market, partnering with Chipotle, Walmart, and Lowe's, providing them with technology to better train employees.

Breaking into the sports industry is no easy feat. Due to the stubbornness that stems from both coaches and front office executives, convincing teams that your product will benefit them can be difficult, especially if it involves new technology.

So, why did Belch experience success so quickly?

To start, he practiced patience during STRIVR's beginning. He used the Stanford team as guinea pigs, ensuring that the product ran smoothly and made sense to the players and coaches before taking the product to market. When he inked a deal with the Cowboys in March, news of the partnership did not break until June. Teams that fell behind were behind, which led to more teams getting over their fears of innovation and signing on to STRIVR, which Belch believes won't be slowing down any time soon.

"Younger coaches and college players coming up are thinking differently and embracing technology more," Belch said. "Everyone understands the value behind it."

* * *

Companies can learn from Belch's experience as an entrepreneur selling his product to professional sports teams. A good business transaction provides benefits to both parties. Yet Belch's recollection of several professional sports teams trying to use their power as a brand to partner with STRIVR for free demonstrates how teams can push startups and entrepreneurs away. Entrepreneurs want to partner with teams, or more broadly companies, that understand the value of their product, not the team with the most championships or the corporation with the largest market share.

Flaunting your brand's legacy to convince an entrepreneur to give you their service for free is not a sustainable strategy in today's innovative climate, especially if the startup recognizes that it has other consumers with higher willingness to pay. In a competitive arena like professional sports, you must put your skin in the game and make a competitive deal.

If you give startups a competitive deal, they will give you a competitive advantage.

Which is exactly why when Leonsis was introduced to STRIVR in the summer of 2015, he pulled the trigger and put together a multiyear partnership with the startup.

The idea was brought forth by an unlikely source. Dan Grunfeld, the son of Washington Wizards General Manager Ernie Grunfeld, played basketball at Stanford and began working at STRIVR as a strategic developer in 2015. He told his father about the technology, who forwarded the message to Leonsis. The Washington sports mogul was immediately sold on the idea, despite the technology being used only for football teams at the time. Leonsis saw the immediate value in the product and did not care about being the first NBA, NHL, and WNBA teams to implement the disruptive technology of virtual reality.

"I put the goggles on and said, 'We got to be the first ones to do this,'" Leonsis explained to The Washington Post in December 2015. Leonsis wanted that first mover advantage.

Zach Leonsis, senior vice president of strategic initiatives at Monumental and son of Ted Leonsis, reiterated this point when asked if there was any level of concern about being the first teams in their respective sports to use virtual reality in training; he said they instead viewed it as a competitive advantage.

"No hesitation," Zach Leonsis emphasized. "We are excited by opportunities to be first to market. That was a plus for us. We saw the applications for team play booking and how are athletes can use it. When you think about a play book, it's like studying for the SAT. To create a visual, complementary tool for studying the playbook was a fabulous opportunity for us to pursue."

A multiyear partnership between Monumental Sports and STRIVR was announced in August 2015. With STRIVR's technology, athletes are able to receive "mental" reps and run through plays without having to exert physical effort.

"The potential competitive advantage that virtual reality training can give us is huge," Capitals defenseman John Carlson said in statement when the partnership was announced.

"STRIVR's experience with football and quarterbacks is exciting for me, because I feel hockey defensemen and quarterbacks go through a similar decision-making process. The virtual reality technology is going to help me fine tune my decision making in games and allow me to train as if I'm at practice without having to be on the ice."

Leonsis' intuition on STRIVR paid off—not just because of the product itself, but because the entire coaching staff and team bought into the idea and were open-minded about the new approach. Perhaps the biggest indication of STRIVR's impact on the organization its effect on the on-ice performance of Braden Holtby, the team's starting goalie.

"We've taken STRIVR out during practice for special teams and goaltending, and individual things like shooting. You want to get the camera closest to a player's visions. We had the players watch the footage in VR. For the goaltenders to watch it and see their own footwork, it's been great," said Capitals video coach Brett Leonhardt, a former goalie himself.

During Holtby's first season as the Capitals starting goalie in 2013-14, he finished with a respectable 2.58 goals allowed average and a .915 save percentage. However, during the 2015-16 season, the first season that STRIVR was implemented into Capitals' practices, Holtby lowered his GAA to an astonishing 2.2—a career best up to that point—and increased his save percentage to .922 while taking home the Veizna Trophy, awarded to the top goaltender in the league.

The implementation of the sports technology in practice translated to in-game success. Though the Capitals secured their first Stanley Cup in June 2018 due to the coaches' and players' hard work and determination throughout the play-offs, the implementation of STRIVR in practices helped sharpen those skills needed to win the Cup.

* * *

As explained earlier by Belch, some sports owners stay away from new technology, citing the traditional aspects of sports and not wanting to mess with older players' routines. However, Ted Leonsis' technology background provided him with an affinity for finding new ways to improve his business and teams, even if it meant disrupting the old-fashioned way of sports training.

"Our players grew up in a video games era, and we believe this method of teaching and sharing of data points will better illustrate what occurs on the court and the ice," Leonsis said in the press release announcing the partnership. Leonsis' evaluation of his players turned out to be true, as the athletes who embraced the technology saw improvements in their performances.

Take Wizards center Ian Mahinmi, for example. Mahinmi signed a four-year, $64 million contract in the 2016 offseason and was expected to make an immediate impact for the Wizards. However, a knee surgery two weeks prior to the start of the season prevented him from spending time on the court. The Wizards coaching staff saw this delay in Mahinmi playing as a perfect opportunity to improve his free-throw shooting percentage, which was slightly below 60%—not great for a professional basketball player. As an eight-year NBA veteran at the time, you could understand and even expect it if Mahinmi would be hesitant to disrupt his routine and try his hand at virtual reality. However, Mahinmi was willing to put aside his any apprehension or bias he might've had and try the new technology.

The Wizards coaches implemented STRIVR's technology by filming Mahinmi's free throws with a 360-degree camera. Mahinmi then put the VR headset on every day to watch his made free throws, coming to understand his mechanics and timing in more detail than traditional film would have allowed.

"It's more like building muscle memory, but for your brain," Mahinmi told ESPN in 2017. "Kind of like, OK, if you see it, your brain is going to register it. And then, when you shoot live, you're going to think about it and see yourself shooting and making. You know you can do it."

The project worked, as Mahinmi hit a career-high 71.7% free-throw shooting percentage when he returned from injury. Mahinmi's teammate, forward Kelly Oubre Jr., also used the virtual reality technology to improve his shooting percentage, which increased from 50.7% to 53.4% after using STRIVR.

But athletes were not the only ones benefiting from Monumental's partnership with STRIVR. As a businessman, Ted Leonsis realized that in order to keep attendance at games relatively high, the arena must also provide opportunities for fan engagement. So, in addition to using the virtual reality technology with his athletes, Leonsis provided fans with the opportunity to use the new technology.

"We also have a strong core of young fans who gravitate to video and gaming, and we believe this technology will resonate with them and increase their engagement with our teams," Ted Leonsis said in the same statement.

Leonsis' son also shared this sentiment, believing that virtual reality would increase the overall fan experience and add value to the brand of Monumental, allowing it to distinguish itself from other ownership groups.

"What's it like to be in the locker room? Or walk down the team tunnel? Or stand courtside during the national anthem?

Virtual reality allows the fans to experience all of these things," Zach Leonsis said.

A month into the 2015-16 season, Monumental opened up a virtual reality station on the lower concourse of the Verizon Center, home to the Capitals, Wizards, and Mystics. During Capitals games, fans were invited to put on the VR headset and take on the role of a goalie. The headset projected an image of Capitals star forward Alex Ovechkin skating toward you. Using a nunchuk controller, fans were tasked with the challenge of stopping a shot from the Russian skater, which would be based on their reaction time. The station increased fan engagement, bringing fans closer than ever to real hockey experiences and their favorite players.

Not only did Leonsis improve player performance, but he also increased fan engagement with his fondness for technology. The virtual reality technology makes the game more interesting for younger fans who grew up watching screens and playing video games, and its implementation in the fan experience increases the value of the in-game fan experience, hopefully leading to lifetime customers or, more importantly, lifetime fans.

* * *

Leonsis' attraction to sports technology startups and potential partnerships did not end with STRIVR. Before the Capitals secured that elusive first Stanley Cup, Leonsis continued looking for ways to improve his team and gain that competitive edge over the competition. Instead of focusing on roster moves to increase the team's potential, Leonsis turned to Kiswe Mobile.

Founded by Dr. Jeong Kim, Jimmy Lynn, and Wim Sweldens in the fall of 2013, Kiswe Mobile focuses on creating an innovative way for fans, specifically millennials, to engage with live sports video content. By offering multiple camera angles, the streaming application allows its users to choose how they want to watch the game while also providing them with real-time statistics and ability to replay any highlights.

"We foresaw the shift in millennials wanting to watch more video on mobile than TV, and the hardest thing to do is to engage with your video on live content and sports, and because it's the most difficult that's what my partners wanted to do," Kiswe co-founder and Vice President Jimmy Lynn said.

Leonsis recognized that he could integrate the tech startups' unique features with his NHL team and approached the company about a potential partnership with the Washington Capitals, which Lynn described as a "no-brainer" to accept, as Kiswe co-founder Dr. Kim is also a partner of the Monumental ownership group. Additionally, Lynn noted Leonsis' desires to be an innovative sports owner.

"Ted has always been an innovative industry leader, going back to his days as president of AOL. Once he bought the teams, he was always regarded as one of the top three owners in the NHL and NBA," Lynn explained. "This ownership group is always trying to push the envelope and try new technology."

Lynn continued to explain his thoughts on why ownership groups of professional sports teams are investing in more and more of these tech companies, comparing it to sports websites during the internet boom.

"When I started AOL in the mid-90s, 1995 was the first year of sports internet sites; my whole pitch was how the internet can drive, develop an incremental revenue stream for you, and now the execs see it in mobile, so it's another way to grow the pot," Lynn said.

On Sept. 13, 2016, about a month before the start of the 2016-17 NHL season, the Washington Capitals officially announced their new partnership with Kiswe Mobile. While the Capitals had used some of Kiswe's features previously, the deal allowed Kiswe to create a service more specific to the Capitals' needs.

"Kiswe's software is a phenomenal teaching tool for our coaching staff and players," Capitals Senior Vice President and General Manager Brian MacLellan said in a statement following the partnership. "Kiswe has made the Capitals a top priority as we have worked to tailor their software to our needs and we look forward to continuing our relationship with them."

This tailored service brought the NHL's top regular-season team a unique competitive advantage.

"We created the ability for them to clip highlights on the bench on two iPads so they could show the players in game during the action," Lynn said. "So, coaches can use them among themselves and show it to the players and also share it with the players between periods and after game. [Capitals Head] Coach [Barry] Trotz said this is a competitive advantage because they had this really cool technology that helped them."

The competitive advantage lies in the ability for Trotz's coaching staff to hone in on specific plays and show multiple camera angles that other teams may not have access to with their normal broadcasting partners to teach their players. The Capitals coaches' ability to not only tell their players what they need to improve upon but to also show them on an iPad provided the players with an extra edge in terms of coachability.

For example, if Trotz wanted to demonstrate to his players where to position themselves on a power play, instead of drawing X's and O's on a whiteboard, Trotz could replay a failed power-play possession, focusing on details away from the puck that the regular television broadcast may have missed. Players are given a more visual representative of what they should be doing on the ice.

Trotz reiterated this advantage in a tweet from Kiswe on Feb. 23, 2017, which quoted the coach as saying, "It's a really advanced tool that every team's gonna need. If they don't have it now, they will."

The NHL caught wind of this technology and announced a deal with Apple during the 2017 Stanley Cup Playoffs, providing each of the 16 postseason teams with iPads and technology similar to what Kiswe provided the Capitals, essentially terminating the competitive advantage that the Capitals had during the regular season.

The partnership with Kiswe showcases Leonsis' willingness as an owner to explore as many options as possible while providing his players with emerging technologies to boost their in-game performances. And, while the advantage attached to the Capitals through Kiswe diminished once the NHL signed the deal with Apple, Leonsis found a way to incorporate it into his next innovative project: Monumental Sports Network.

* * *

"The next-generation sports fan."

A phrase mentioned more than once during a phone call with Zach Leonsis. A phrase that cracks open the door into the future. A phrase that explains the objective of decisions made by Monumental Sports & Entertainment, as they try to target the next-generation sports fan, now.

Zach Leonsis believes that strategic media decisions are essential for appealing to the younger fan base. So, instead of solely relying on regional sports networks, which require fans to subscribe to cable to watch live games and team-related content, the younger Leonsis helped Monumental launch its own over-the-top media platform, called Monumental Sports Network.

"From our perspective, half of our companies' revenue nowadays come from media dollars, and those media dollars are driven through people's subscriptions," Leonsis explained. "My big project a couple of years ago was our regional sports broadcasting partnership with Comcast and NBC Sports. Something that alarmed us was that over the lifetime of our deal with NBC, our numbers of subscribers to the network would be declining at the time while our region [population] is scheduled to increase. That was alarming for us, because our building sells out every night, and if you can't get into the building you have to rely on cable. It's important for us to be available on a variety of platforms and channels so our teams can be exposed to the next generation of fans."

Monumental Sports Network launched Oct. 11, 2016. Through the subscription-based service, fans are treated to live games for the WNBA Washington Mystics, AFL Washington Valor, AHL Hershey Bears, and numerous high school sporting events. While Washington Capitals and Wizards games are not available to be streamed on the platform due to NHL and NBA broadcasting rights, Monumental Sports Network provides in-depth coverage of both teams, including a live midday show dedicated to both teams.

Despite the fact that both the Wizards and Capitals have a long-term, advanced media partnership with NBC Sports Groups, Leonsis views the formation of the Monumental Sports Network as a long-term solution; he hopes to stay ahead of the curve of other professional sports teams when cord-cutting diminishes cable's existence and OTT digital platforms become the norm for entertainment viewing.

"We are very much in the media business; we think of ourselves to be in the media business. [In terms of] streaming technologies, we are one of the only teams out there that has their own OTT direct-to-consumer platform," Leonsis said.

What makes Monumental Sports Network's platform so appealing to younger viewers is the use of Kiswe's technology to incorporate interactive elements into the stream. Viewers are able to choose between multiple camera angles to watch, immediately share clips on social media, and get access to real-time stats right on the screen. This provides the younger fan with a much more engaged platform than what a traditional cable package can offer, which is a single camera angle determined by the broadcaster with no immediate access to highlights.

While Monumental Sports Network provided a solution for the future of sports broadcasting, it has also opened the door for other opportunities that can benefit the organization as it targets younger fans. Leonsis knew that Monumental Sports Network had to diversify the content it offers while still appealing to the next generation of sports fans. Leonsis had to ask himself what type of content younger viewers wanted to see, and the answer was in video games.

Twenty years ago, if someone said that they wanted to become a professional video game player, they would get laughed at and told to dedicate their time to something other than video games. However, that sentiment has drastically shifted as electronic sports, or eSports, has gained more popularity and turned into a cash cow, generating $1.5 billion in global revenue in 2017. And now, eSports has caught the attention of professional sports teams across the globe.

"I spent about two years trying to figure out how we could participate in eSports," Leonsis admitted. "There was also an audience exploding, with 50 million people watching championship events, but none of them were paying subscriptions like a traditional cable model. Instead, all of them were exposed to brand advertising and opting to subscribe to support a player or team on their own. We found it was very interesting from a media perspective and saw it as an opportunity to learn from."

Leonsis saw eSports as the perfect event to stream on Monumental Sports Network. A majority of eSports content was already consumed on digital platforms, such as Twitch but, as Leonsis said, did not require subscriptions. ESports competitions are the first live sporting event that relies on digital streams as its primary broadcasting platform. ESports provides Monumental Sports Network with the potential winning idea for OTT sports streaming services; all they needed now was an eSports team to stream, which would require a heavy investment.

"From our perspective, we don't necessarily want to get into a lot of venture, investment opportunities because more likely then not they don't work," Leonsis explained. "If we see an opportunity that we genuinely think will increase the value of our business, or improve performance, and we will do as much for the company as they will be doing for us. We also like to invest in opportunities that we think are ahead of their time and bracing for the future and feed into our thesis of the next-generation sports fan."

From an investment standpoint, an eSports team ticked off all of the right boxes for Monumental. It would increase its value as a business, providing it with an additional revenue stream and added value to Monumental Sports Network, while also helping the ownership group focus in on younger consumers.

In September 2016, Monumental Sports & Entertainment teamed up with Mandalay Entertainment Group, which is led by Golden State Warriors, LA Dodgers, and LA FC co-owner Peter Gruber to form aXiomatic—an investment group dedicated to the eSports industry.

On Sept. 27, 2016, aXiomatic announced its first investment, acquiring a majority stake in Team Liquid, an eSports team that Leonsis described as the "New York Yankees" of professional gaming. While the investment group did not disclose the financial details of the deal, you can assume they paid a hefty price, considering Team Liquid is the current top-earning eSports franchise, pulling in a total of $18,957,637.34 in prize money since its 2000 founding.

"When we got the opportunity to invest in Team Liquid, we did because we wanted a brand that was authentic in the eSports community. We wanted to fund operators who we trusted and liked because we knew if we tried to come out with our own eSports team, it wouldn't go well. We knew we needed serious operators who already knew the space, understood market dynamics, and we found that," Leonsis explained.

Because aXiomatic was new to the eSports space, the group decided to keep Team Liquid former owners Steve Archancet and Victor Goossens on as co-CEOs. Because both were former professional gamers themselves, Ted Leonsis decided it was in the team's best interest to allow them to continue running the team.

"My belief, and Peter Guber's belief—we came at this separately and we both ended up at the same place; that's why we ended up splitting the team, if you will—was that people like Steve, people like Victor, were real," Ted Leonsis said in an interview with Pete Volk in November 2016. "They were respected, they were a part of this organic growth, and it was better for us to reward them, invest in them, leave them alone around the game and the competitiveness itself. I'm never going to tell them who to hire as a coach, what players to recruit, what the training regiment should be; I just wouldn't do that."

While Monumental Sports Network currently does not have streaming rights to Team Liquid events, it does offer coverage of the team, providing fans inside looks at their favorite professional gamers as they ready themselves for competitions. It also provides Monumental Sports & Entertainment a safety net for the future, if the popularity of traditional sports start to decline.

"I think very quickly eSports will be the largest participatory sport, business, industry, with the most active participants, the most dollars, compared to any sport," Ted Leonsis told The Washington Post in December 2016. "It will dwarf the NFL. It will dwarf the NBA, because first and foremost it is a global phenomenon. China, Korea, all of the Asian nations, they are early adopters there first."

Monumental Sports & Entertainment was also the first professional sports ownership group to appoint a director for its eSports division, having hired Grant Paranjape to head its other eSports investment: an NBA 2K League team. As the first eSports league to be co-owned by a professional sports organization, the NBA 2K League will host a four-month season during which 17 NBA team-affiliated eSports teams will compete with one another on the popular basketball video game platform for a prize pool of $1 million.

These investments in the eSports industry open up the door for Monumental to acquire streaming rights for live eSports event in the future, if it can maintain the success of Team Liquid and provide eSports fans with the coverage they want. Monumental Sports & Entertainment's investment in the eSports industry is a move for the future, not the present, as it attempts to acquire the next generation of sports fans as lifetime consumers.

* * *

Innovation is a team sport, and strong leadership is integral when managing innovation. Business leaders should take note of Leonsis' attraction and dedication to innovation. Rather than running away from new technologies—like the 10 NFL teams that rejected Belch's pitch for STRIVR at the draft—Leonsis sets an example for his employees by embracing technological advances and promoting innovation among his employees, coaches, and players.

The same can be applied to businesses in other industries. No matter the case, there will always be executives who will stand by the "old-fashioned" way of running a business, refusing to integrate technology into their teams due to prejudice. But those who succeed are the business leaders who challenge the norm by taking innovative risks to increase the value of their assets.

It is also worth discussing Leonsis' approach to these partnerships. As Belch stated during his interview, he found it difficult to work with some NFL teams due to their unwillingness to put forth capital in exchange for his product. In other words, they did not put skin in the game and, as a result, fell behind those teams that took the risk of giving Belch a competitive offer to demonstrate their perceived valuation of STRIVR. While the financial details are not disclosed, Leonsis' offer to Belch was strong enough for him to agree with it and provide all of the teams under Monumental Sports & Entertainment with STRIVR products.

Leonsis' commitment to technology has proven how professional sports teams can practice "continuous innovation" without creating a dedicated incubator or accelerator program. Through a partnership with STRIVR, Leonsis unlocked the disruptive technology of virtual reality, becoming the first owner in the NHL, NBA, and WNBA to adopt this new method of training. The formation of aXiomatic and the acquisition of Team Liquid put Monumental in a prime position to take advantage of the rise in popularity of eSports and the potential of the emerging sport.

Through strategic partnerships and investments, Leonsis has demonstrated that an effective way to promote entrepreneurial thinking and corporate innovation throughout his ownership group is by not fearing the uncertainty associated with being a first mover. In fact, Leonsis embraces it. And now he has a Stanley Cup to prove that it works.

CHAPTER 6

SMART IN SPOTS

———

"Learning and innovation go hand in hand. The arrogance of success is to think that what you did yesterday will be sufficient for tomorrow."

—WILLIAM POLLARD

Snake.

Traitor.

Cupcake.

Words basketball fans used to describe Kevin Durant and voice their displeasure with the 2014 NBA Most Valuable Player's decision to leave the Oklahoma City Thunder to join the Golden State Warriors as a free agent during the 2016 offseason.

Durant's decision disgusted NBA fans not because he left the franchise that drafted him in 2007, but rather because he joined the Warriors, a team fresh off a record-breaking 73-win campaign that featured a lineup of two-time MVP Steph Curry, four-time all-star Klay Thompson, and three-time all-star Draymond Green. Durant's decision to jump ship and join the Warriors disrupted the competitive balance of the league and solidified a "dynasty" team in every sense of the word, as the Warriors have now won the NBA championship in both seasons with Durant.

As angry as I am about his decision to join perhaps the most hated team in the league (unless you live in the Bay Area), another word can be used to describe Kevin Durant and his decision to sign with the Warriors.

Genius.

The average fan may not realize that Durant's move to the Bay Area was more than just a basketball decision. It was also a business decision. While Durant's top priority was to bring another championship to Oakland, the former MVP also wanted to build his business portfolio through investments from his venture capital firm, the Durant Company; signing with the Warriors placed him in the epicenter of tech and innovation: Silicon Valley.

Durant's decision to move out to the West Coast—and, more specifically, Silicon Valley—makes more sense when put into the context of the emerging trend of athletes investing in tech startups and other business ventures to boost their off-court brand and credibility.

High-profile athletes such as LeBron James and Carmelo Anthony have led the charge in what it means to be an athlete-investor. Despite not being investors by trade, James' and Anthony's willingness to learn about the world of investments has opened multiple doors for their careers after the NBA. And not only do these investments benefit the athletes, but these companies have also received increased exposure due to these high-profile investors and have devised how to strategically incorporate the athlete-investors into their business operations.

Athlete-investors bring an innovative approach to how emerging startups can gain traction early on, but only if they are strong enough ideas to get former MVPs to take a financial stake in the company. Yet once that's secured, how the startups handle these unique investors opens many opportunities to better engage with their customers and promote their products.

*　*　*

LeBron James has achieved many great feats on the basketball court. During his first 14 years in the National Basketball Association, James has claimed three NBA championships, four MVP awards, and 14 consecutive trips to the All-Star Game. Yet it seems James' smartest accomplishment has been off the court and in the form of an assist by his financial adviser, Paul Wachter.

In 2012, Wachter introduced James to Rick and Elise Wetzel, the founders of Blaze Pizza. Founded in 2011, Blaze Pizza was a brand new pizza chain that bakes personalized pizzas in an assembly line, similar to Chipotle's operations. James was immediately on board with the idea of becoming an original investor, which took Rick Wetzel by surprise.

"I didn't think I could do it," Rick Wetzel admitted when asked about his reaction to learning that James was a potential investor. "I thought he was too big for us. But it turned out that he was quite humble and really liked the idea, so we were being more humble ourselves and thinking, 'Oh we're not ready for that,' but we were, apparently, because LeBron thought so."

But this was not the first time that James strategically invested in emerging brands. When Beats Headphones were first introduced to the public in 2008, the company offered an innovative alternative to headphones currently on the market, focusing on combining aspects of fashion and high-quality sound to the product's development. The challenge came in trying to convince casual music listeners that these headphones were worth the expensive price tag.

Instead of recruiting athletes to sign endorsement deals with the brand, Beats offered James a "small stake" in the company as compensation for promoting the use of headphones. During the following seasons, James would be seen walking into arenas, dressed in a suit with Beats Headphones over his ears, spreading brand awareness and persuading consumers to try the product. And when Apple purchased Beats for $3 billion in 2014, James received what is believed to be the largest single equity payout for an athlete, a return of $30 million, just for wearing headphones and appearing in a few TV spots.

Securing one of the greatest basketball players of all time as an original investor aided Blaze Pizza's success, especially during the company's early stages. In 2013—about a year into James' investment—Blaze Pizza racked up a total of $6 million in sales, which skyrocketed to $33 million the following year. High-profile athletes are powerful investors, because they can influence all their fans and followers to try new things, especially things they have invested in, as it adds credibility to the brand.

"To have a celebrity involved in your organization is that when you're young and not a known entity, it lets others take more notice of you," Wetzel explained. "Initially, it just helps to put you on the field a little stronger by having them involved in the business. Completely aside from anything they would do, it's just the fact that they are attached to it. It makes people sit up and go, 'Oh, this looks like it might be credible; what is it?' and they just look a little harder at it."

By attaching itself to James' personal brand, mainly through his social media influence, Blaze experienced rapid growth and success due to the credibility it gave the new, emerging company.

In October 2015, James augmented Blaze Pizza's credibility further in a shocking move when he declined a $15 million endorsement deal with McDonald's to continue his partnership with Blaze. James walked away from the McDonald's deal, allowing himself to further invest in Blaze while also fully committing his marketing power to the pizza joint.

"I believe in the company. I believe in their vision. I believe in what they're all about, the authenticity of how they make pizza, how they run their business, and I wanted to be a part of it," James said in an ESPN interview in 2015.

In the past, athletes have turned to their personal brands to make money off the court, offering their services to brands through endorsement deals. James turning down an endorsement deal may not seem like a big deal, but considering that endorsement deals were the industry norm at the time, the King's decision marked a dramatic shift in how athletes can use their personal brand to gain greater monetary returns off the court.

The problem with traditional endorsement deals is that they offer no incentive other than the fixed sum owed in the contract to motivate the athlete to advocate for a brand. Athletes do not have to do much other than appear in commercials and read off a script. There is a lack of personal belief behind these brand messages. Whenever I see Chris Paul in a State Farm commercial, I think to myself, "Does he actually care about insurance agencies, or does Paul just want to see another check deposited in his bank account?"

It is thus better not only for the brands but for the athletes themselves, becoming investors rather than getting paid for their superficial endorsements. As an investor, an athlete has more control over what they can say, how they can promote the brand, and the amount of return on their investment. In other words, athletes who are investors typically get out what they put in. If an athlete is like LeBron, an individual who truly believes in the company's vision and shows it on social media and when visiting chains, then their commitment to the brand will be noticed by the public, therefore increasing the value of the brand, which, in turn, increases the value of the athlete's investment.

While the total amount of the investment was not revealed, a source told ESPN that James owned more than 10% equity in the pizza chain. While his money has opened many opportunities for the then-early stage company, James' presence on social media perhaps influenced the success of Blaze Pizza the most.

"He will chat about us on his social media, which is where he's really helpful. When he's out on the road, he'll pop into one of the restaurants, buy pizza for people. He helps to keep our awareness up. We call him an ambassador of the brand because he is so high-profile," Wetzel said.

James has wielded his social media presence to demonstrate his passion for Blaze Pizza. Boasting 35.7 million followers on Instagram to couple with his 40 million Twitter followers, James is among social media's elite class and uses that as an opportunity to promote his favorite pizza chain. After enjoying a meal at Blaze Pizza on April 2, 2016, James decided to capture his customized pizza, as well as the aftermath—a lack of leftovers—and share it on Instagram. The post received 170,356 likes along with 3,106 comments, highlighting the level of engagement celebrity endorsements incur. Wetzel shared one of his favorite sayings and how it applied to James' role with the company.

"I have a sticky note on my wall that says, 'I'm smart in spots, and I stay around those spots,' and all of us up here do that," Wetzel said. "There are things that each of us are good at, and we tend to work in those areas and avoid the areas where we are not good. LeBron is a very good partner, and he does the things that matter, and he doesn't get into the stuff that's not his strong point. He loves the brand; he'll talk about how proud he is to be a founding investor in the company, and on that level it's very strong. "

If you stopped by the Blaze Pizza location in Pasadena, California, during the lunch rush on March 11, 2016, you may have noticed that one of the Blaze Pizza employees was not like the others.

"You look very familiar. Very familiar," one customer told the worker.

"He looks like Dwayne Wade!" another customer told their friend.

The employee *did look familiar, but he was not Dwayne Wade. He was LeBron James.*

On an off day, James took on the alter ego "Ron" to help out at the ingredients line and exchange playful banter with unsuspecting customers. Once people caught on to the act, their reactions were priceless: They were dumbfounded that one of the greatest athletes of our generation was making their pizza. As an ambassador of the brand, James offers an innovative approach to what it means to promote an ad. Rather than appearing in 30-second ads or billboards, James interacts with the consumers of the brand in a more direct and empathetic manner that can be used to build lifetime customer value. As a consumer, would you rather buy from a brand because LeBron told you to through a screen or from a brand that LeBron believes in so much that he devotes his time to work behind the counter and truly live the brand?

Blaze Pizza opened its 200th franchise July 11, 2017, making it the fastest growing restaurant chain in history. Blaze Pizza CEO Jim Mizes projected that the company can go public as early as 2020, with a goal of securing a billion-dollar evaluation. Much of Blaze Pizza's rapid success can be owed to James and how committed he has been to the success of the company. Wetzel could not have been happier about how this partnership worked out.

"You couldn't pick a better celebrity to be attached to," Wetzel emphasized. "His stature is growing, and he's got great character. He's just doing real smart things that make his brand go bigger and more attractive."

Professional athletes' greatest assets to entrepreneurs include not just their net worth but also the credibility attached to their personal brand. For an athlete as famous as James, his social influence has greater potential to significantly increase the public's awareness of a brand than any traditional form of endorsements, especially when the brand promotes an innovative idea that may not be widely accepted by mass markets. Having your investors become your key brand ambassadors saves the startup a great deal in marketing costs.

Furthermore, James' humility has allowed Blaze Pizza to continue to dominate the fast-casual restaurant market. Rather than offering business advice regarding strategy or operations, like other investors may do, James is aware of his own strengths, knowing that he is more valuable to the company as an "ambassador to the brand" than as a business consultant.

James' investment also represents a shift away from the traditional endorsement deals, such as his previous deal with McDonald's. Rather than renewing the endorsement deal with the fast-food chain, James passed on this opportunity to bet more money on Blaze Pizza's future. Investing in startups is an innovative method for athletes to endorse brands, and more athletes should follow James' path. Investments can lead to much greater returns than endorsement deals but require hard work and more commitment to the brand on the athlete's part. If an athlete believes in the brand strongly, as James does with Blaze Pizza, they can see the value of their investment increase as they spread their message and become more motivated to be strong in their spots.

* * *

It was just another day at the boxing gym for Stuart Goldfarb.

The former NBC executive turned investor was finishing up another tough workout when he struck up a conversation with his friend Alani. Realizing that he did not know too much about his workout buddy, he asked her about her husband.

"He's Carmelo Anthony," Alani responded.

"Who?" Goldfarb replied, quizzical.

"You know, the Knicks player?"

Just like that, Goldfarb learned the name of his future business partner, despite not knowing anything about the NBA all-star. Apparently, Goldfarb is not a huge basketball fan. But he soon became a huge Carmelo Anthony fan.

At the time Anthony was not just any Knicks player. Since arriving to the team in 2012, Anthony had led the Knicks in scoring in each of his seven seasons in New York, in addition to winning the Knicks' first division title in 19 years in 2013 and finishing seventh on the franchise's all-time scoring list.

At the same time, Anthony discovered the true value of technology and what it means to be innovative in today's society. During the 2012-13 season, the New York Knicks introduced wearable technology into their training regimen. Through a partnership with Australian sports technology company Catapult Sports, the Knicks provided each player with the OptimEye, a small sensor attached to the back of a player's jersey. The sensor tracks a player's movements in a 3D space, collecting data such as acceleration of movements, force of movements, and changes in cardiovascular activity. Anthony was dumbfounded by the applications that technology could have not just on the basketball court but in every aspect of life. He was immediately on board with meeting Goldfarb, and a friendship quickly developed.

"I didn't know who her husband was. And she said, 'Oh come on, you will really like him; why don't you come to a party?'" Goldfarb recalled with embarrassment. "It was during basketball season, and I'd come over to their house, drink wine on off days, and just talk [with Anthony] about different businesses. At the time I [had] been, for the past 10 to 15 years, doing angel investing in a very casual way. We started talking about technology and athletics and really texting until like midnight, one o'clock in the morning, with all sorts of ideas."

So, during the 2013 NBA offseason, Anthony and Goldfarb visited several startups in New York and California, and Anthony expressed enthusiasm about working with Goldfarb. At the beginning, Anthony viewed this project as a learning experience, aware of his own lack of business expertise and eager to learn more about the tech industry.

"For me, it was more about learning the business, not just jumping in there and investing my money but learning the business," Anthony described during a 2016 TechCrunch panel . "And I'm still learning the business, learning how to read a business plan, learning the difference between a bad business plan and a good business plan."

As Anthony gained more knowledge of the opportunities that tech investments could bring, he suddenly realized the end goal of these meetings. Rather than being a consumer of technology, Anthony wanted to become more involved with innovative concepts and brand himself as "the digital athlete."

On the court, Anthony realized the potential of innovative technology in the world of sports. However, it was his idea for off-the-court use that made him want to invest in other companies. Instead of restricting its usage to sports teams, Anthony believed the OptimEye could be repositioned and marketed to a wider market of non-athletes. While he did not get to share his thoughts with Catapult Sport's executive team, Anthony knew he wanted to do the same for other startups and make an impact in the world.

"When you first get into the tech game, you start reading and become more aware of the business model of the tech world," Anthony noted. "What's doing this? What's doing that? How much money is being spent in the tech industry? And you want to be a part of that someway, somehow. You are always thinking about: 'How can I just have that one time where I just hit a home run?' But then as you start putting things into perspective, you really have to take your time; you really have to understand the game. 'What can I do to be a part of the ever-changing world on a day-to-day business?'—and that was kind of one of the reasons I wanted to be involved in tech."

While the duo made some investments during their 2013 tour, Melo7 Tech Partners wasn't officially launched until July 2014. As an investment firm, Melo7 Tech Partners does not limit itself to one industry. Its current portfolio is highly diversified, funding technology startups serving a wide variety of sectors, such as sports, fashion, and food. The firm's first investment was in Hullabalu, a startup redefining traditional children's storytelling by introducing interactive stories with which kids can engage on tablets and mobile devices. As a parent, Anthony saw the value in the startup and wanted its vision to be heard.

"Everybody wants to be heard. Everybody has a voice, and I think technology gives everyone the opportunity to be heard," Anthony said about why he dedicates his investments to tech companies.

The second startup in which Melo7 Tech Partners invested in led to a hefty payday for the basketball player and his co-investor. Melo7 Tech Partners participated in Whistle's Series A funding in June 2013 and again during the startup's Series B round in January 2015. Whistle—described as the "Fit-Bit for dogs"—produced high-tech dog collars that tracked a pet's fitness activity and rest periods. Three years after Melo7 invested in the startup, Mars Petcare acquired the company for a rumored $100 million. But the point wasn't the money for Anthony, whose 2017-18 NBA salary was a substantial $26 million. The point was the ride.

"The money is enticing, but it's also the thrill of being involved in companies that are changing the world today," Anthony clarified. "Tech is changing the world, whether it's sports, fashion, music. Regardless of what it is, it's changing the world, so how can I become better at knowing what is going on out there and being a part of that world."

The investment game, however, isn't always smooth sailing. A study conducted by Sports Illustrated back in 2009 showed that 60% of NBA players go broke within five years of retirement. While some of that can be attributed to extravagant spending, much of their multimillion-dollar career earnings are lost in bad investments.

"They don't know how they're invested. They don't know what they're doing. They don't know if they're being overcharged on fees. They have no clue," said Carlos Dias, a wealth manager for MVP Wealth Management. "They just have somebody that's 'their guy.'"

The key difference for Anthony was his attempt to understand and learn how his money was being invested, while still keeping his day job.

"When you look at athletes, even athletes who have built very strong personal brands, there are very few whose brands have survived their athletic career," Goldfarb stated. "I think there are a lot of reasons for it, and I think one of the main ones is that they don't think about building a brand that's going to be different from their career until their career is over, which is kind of too late."

Anthony's success as an investor derives from his commitment to innovation and willingness to take his role as an investor seriously, while still playing in the NBA rather than waiting for retirement. Through the introduction of wearable technology to him as a player, Anthony realized the impact tech startups can have not only in sports but also in all aspects of everyday life. Anthony recognized that he could not pass up the opportunity to learn from a seasoned investor like Goldfarb and knew he needed a mentor if he wanted to do this right. As for the future of Melo7 Tech Partners, Anthony does not plan on slowing down anytime soon.

"This is something that is a long-term plan for me," Anthony said. "It is not something I'm just in for one year, two years, [or] I'm just trying to get into one company and become more rich off of just one company. This is something I see myself doing now and way beyond my career."

* * *

In 353 words, Kevin Durant shocked the NBA and sports world. Through an open letter published on The Player's Tribune on July 4, 2016, Durant announced his decision to join the Golden State Warriors. While many were quick to point out that his reasoning behind the decision had to do with his desire to win his first NBA championship—and win it quickly—the other reasoning could be found in an ambiguous sentence from his letter.

"I am also at a point in my life where it is of equal importance to find an opportunity that encourages my evolution as a man: moving out of my comfort zone to a new city and community which offers the greatest potential for my contribution and personal growth," Durant penned in his letter.

The new community was Silicon Valley, and the potential for his contribution and personal growth lay in his desire to get involved in tech investments.

The idea sprouted in Durant's mind during his trip to San Francisco to watch the Super Bowl L. While driving to the stadium, Durant, along with his business manager and agent Rich Kleiman, passed by the Postmates office. Durant, an avid user of Postmates due to his traveling schedule during the season, suggested that they pop in then and there. Kleiman offered to set up a meeting at a later date instead. The meeting resulted in an investment of under $1 million, which was not announced until later that summer, when Durant fully immersed himself into the Postmates brand, biking around New York City, delivering his latest Nike shoes to lucky customers.

While Durant signed a 10-year, $300 million endorsement deal with Nike in 2014, he stated his preference for investments in an 2018 ESPN interview.

"The only thing we aren't doing is endorsement deals," Durant said. "There's nothing wrong with them, but time is the most important thing to me. And when you endorse a product, a lot of your time is taken away."

Similar to James' role with Blaze Pizza, Durant prefers to throw his weight behind these startups in which he has invested and for which he believes he can create a deeper connection to both the brand and the brand's consumers, through investments rather than endorsements.

"Even though I may not be there every day, I feel like I've left my imprint on things. So I'd rather do that than be an endorser of something, where I'm having to do commercials and photo shoots and go to events," Durant admitted. "I just want to believe in someone else, that they have a great idea, and try to back it as much as I can financially. And if they do need a little push from me, you know, I'm not saying I'm the biggest name in sports or in the entertainment business, but a lot of people follow me on social media and a lot of people know and watch basketball."

Currently, the Durant Company holds a number of investments in tech startups offering consumer-facing products. According to its website, the company has invested in Acorn, a micro-investing app; Coinbase, a digital currency exchange; The Player's Tribune, the Derek Jeter-founded media platform for athletes; and Blaze Pizza's competitor Pieology (he's coming for you, LeBron!).

Like Anthony, Durant had to do a lot of homework before setting up meetings and investing his own money. Like Anthony, Durant was aware of his lack of investment knowledge and, like Anthony, surrounded himself with mentors, such as Warriors owner Joe Lacob (a partner at VC firm Kleiner Perkins Caufield & Byers), Ben Horowitz (co-founder of VC firm Andreessen Horowitz), and Ron Conway (early-stage angel investor for Google and PayPal). When he sits in a room full of these powerful, successful investors, Durant realizes that his NBA accomplishments do not translate to the business world.

"You have to remove the ego of it and realize that you don't know it all," Durant explained. "I want to learn more about this life and this business and this world. So, I've got to ask questions, and I've got to have an open mind to it all."

As an investor, Durant is smart in spots and stays in those spots. For Durant, his strength is mainly in the form of promotional activity—not as a brand ambassador, but rather an ambassador of the brand who lives, speaks, and walks the values of the company every day. For example, when he invested in Rubrik, a business-to-business cloud data management service, he also agreed to become a board adviser for the startup, focusing his efforts on branding.

With business-to-consumer startups, Durant's presence as an NBA star is enough to generate excitement among a brand's consumer base. During the 2018 NBA Finals, Postmates raffled off two free tickets to Game 2 in Oakland, urging users to employ the code "KD" to enter the contest while also emphasizing Durant's role in its team as an investor. Postmates utilized Durant's appearance in the NBA Finals and the popularity of the sport as leverage to drive more downloads and encourage in-app purchases.

When asked what the best business advice he received was, Durant kept his answer short and emulated Anthony's approach to investments.

"Don't do things just for money. Don't do things just for fame. Do things because you feel right and it feels true," Durant said.

Athletes should not do endorsement deals for the money. Athletes should involve themselves with brands they believe in and would support financially through investments—and corporations looking to innovate their marketing strategies regarding athletes should take note.

* * *

While their NBA career achievements are distinct, Carmelo Anthony, LeBron James, and Kevin Durant share several characteristics that make them ideal investors. Aside from being drafted just one spot away from each other in the 2003 NBA Draft, James and Anthony both recognize the value and potential of investing in innovative startups. Whether it's a new way to listen to music while looking cool or a delivery service that brings food right to your door, these three NBA stars identify products and ideas they truly believe in and use that sense of personal belief to deliver strong brand messages.

But it's not as easy as just throwing your money at a company. Especially for a company that offers a unique product or service, it could take time for the public to widely accept it. High-profile investors must understand their core strengths and consider how they can apply those strengths to become better investors. If you are struggling to determine your own personal strengths, do not be afraid to discuss it with partners or past coworkers.

For James, it is his awareness of his social influence, allowing him to tap into his wealth of social media followers to encourage others to try new brands. In Anthony's case, his strength has more to do with his willingness to learn and pay close attention to Goldfarb's advice, thus acquiring more business knowledge through his mentor. And for Durant, it's about doing what you believe is in your best interest without worrying what others will say.

The promotion and acceptance of innovative ideas allows a firm to gain credibility with the public. High-profile investors are a key source of more effective marketing tactics, especially considering their returns are correlated to the success of the company. If the high-profile investor wants to gain higher returns, they will commit the time and effort necessary to sell the idea of the business and gain mass market acceptance.

And, while Anthony may never compete with how many championships James or Durant have won, maybe one day he can brag about how his investments are doing better than those of the former MVPs.

CHAPTER 7

PRIMING FOR SUCCESS

"Creativity is thinking up new things. Innovation is doing new things."

— THEODORE LEVITT

"The Flip."

Two words guaranteed to put a smile on a New York Yankees fan's face, referring to the play that solidified Derek Jeter's status as a Yankees' legend just six years into his professional career.

It was the seventh inning of Game 3 of the 2001 ALDS, with the Yankees holding a tight 1-0 lead over the Oakland Athletics. With a runner on first base, the Athletics' Terrence

Long drove a hit down the right field foul line. Yankees out-fielder Shane Spencer hustled to the ball and, knowing that the runner from first would try to score, threw the ball back into the infield as hard as he could, missing two cutoff men on the way.

Just when it seemed like Oakland would tie the game, a sprinting Jeter came out of nowhere, cutting off the ball 10 feet in front of home plate and flipping it to Yankees catcher Jorge Posada, who applied the tag on the runner. The play preserved the Yankees' lead, which they would hold on to and use to ultimately win the series.

What makes "The Flip" more memorable than Jeter's other moments is the sheer fact that a play like that has never been done before (and has not been done since). It was creative. It was unique.

Haters will say the play was lucky, arguing Jeter was in the right place at the right time. However, Jeter is a shortstop and should usually be nowhere near home plate, especially on the right side of the baseball diamond. As the play developed, Jeter quickly identified a gap in the field that needed to be filled and positioned himself in a spot that would give the Yankees what they needed: an out.

But what does any of this have to do with business?

Engaging in innovative business practices can be frightening at first, especially if a corporation takes the route of innovating externally through accelerators, capital investments, partnerships, or mergers and acquisitions. Because the innovative assets come in externally the corporation must determine how to integrate these new operations into its corporate culture and business functions.

Innovation is a high-risk decision with potential for a high reward. Jeter's play was risky: He could have missed his catcher completely, allowing the runner to score, prolonging the inning, and gifting the Athletics with a chance to come back in the series. Yet Jeter positioned himself for success by identifying a hole in his team's defense and gravitating toward it.

Risks are inevitable. There can always be a downside to any decision you make, whether in business, sports, or your everyday life. But the mere potential for risks cannot be a source of discouragement, as there are methods to prime your innovative idea for success and mitigate risks. For firms striving to provide innovative products and services, perhaps the best way to reduce risk is to understand your consumers' wants and needs and to ensure that those consumer desires are met, especially in the Digital Age, when consumers are getting more innovative in how they want to consume products.

While LeBron James and Carmelo Anthony are busy meeting with potential startups to invest in, Jeter—as well as Steph Curry—has taken matters into his own hands, founding startups able to directly address the needs of consumers who are innovative in how they consume these products. While Jeter's venture paints a picture of how developing a methodical plan of attack allows firms to test the market and position themselves for success prior to a launch, Curry's entrepreneurial experiences demonstrate how firms can handle failure and resposition themselves for success by pivoting.

* * *

When a 21-year-old Derek Jeter was called up by the New York Yankees to make his MLB debut, he immediately faced two great challenges: The first was that he would be the starting shortstop for one of the most storied franchises in all of sports, and secondly, he would be playing in New York City, which he described as the "toughest media environment in all of sports" following his retirement in 2014.

Despite being marked as the savior of the franchise so early in his career, Jeter kept a cool head during his time in pinstripes and was known around the sports media world as a "quiet" athlete who attempted to avoid the spotlight, especially when controversies arose.

For example, when the New York Yankees traded for Alex Rodriguez prior to the 2004 season, the New York media went into a frenzy with the breaking news, pointing back to a comment made by Rodriguez to Esquire in 2001.

"Jeter's been blessed with great talent around him," Rodriguez stated in the interview. "He's never had to lead."

Despite the belittling comment, Jeter never displayed his thoughts and feelings on personal matters directly to the press. Even with the New York sports media trying to make the most of a controversial situation, Jeter never spoke poorly of Rodriguez to reporters.

"If I was giving headlines all the time, I wouldn't have been here for 20 years," Jeter asserted in a New York Magazine cover story from 2014.

In a more humorous situation, the New York Post published a piece in December 2011 claiming that the Yankees' legend provided his one-night stands with a car service the next morning along with a gift basket of signed memorabilia. While many athletes would immediately turn to social media or call up a reporter to deny such claims, Jeter chose a different approach and waited three years to address the issue.

"Like I'm giving them signed baseballs and pictures of myself on the way out! Who comes up with a story like that?" Jeter said laughingly in the same cover story.

Addressing the controversies when they first arose may have provided a short-term solution by allowing him to tell his side of the story, but Jeter realized that there would be more costs than benefits in the long run if he took this route.

In an interview with Joe Buck in November 2015, Jeter defended his decision to ignore the rumor and not feed into its lies.

"I don't address them because once you address it, you have to address every single rumor that comes out," Jeter explained. "And then if one time you don't, they automatically assume it's true."

Stories like these demonstrate the dangers of journalists for athletes. Jeter realized that if he talked about these issues when they first appeared, more and more headlines would pop up, allowing the "true" story to be based on the author's interpretation of Jeter's hypothetical denial. So, instead, Jeter choose the option that he perceived to be more beneficial to his career and decided to keep quiet and let the rumors die down.

* * *

When it was ready for "The Captain" to call it quits, Jeter opted out of the traditional press conference to announce his retirement and instead turned to social media to say what he wanted to say. Prior to the start of the 2014 season, Jeter published a 725-word Facebook post to announce that the upcoming season would be his last. It was a creative approach to retirement, especially for a future Hall of Famer, as Jeter became the first high-profile athlete to announce their retirement through social media.

Rather than hosting a press conference and leaving it to the reporters to craft click-bait headlines based on carefully selected soundbites, Jeter wanted to do it his own way, in his own words, making sure everyone knew that retirement was his decision. By laying it all on the table in a well-written letter, Jeter left little room for outside interpretations.

For the first time in 20 years, Jeter finally gave the media the headline they wanted. In his final at-bat at Yankee Stadium, Jeter did what he did best in his Yankee uniform: smacking a walk-off single to right field. But the real headline came from his postgame conference, in which a normally calm, collected Jeter delivered an emotional interview, admitting that he had to take multiple bathroom breaks throughout the game to prevent himself from tearing up on camera.

But the headlines did not stop there.

On Oct. 1, 2014—just three days after his final MLB game—
Jeter announced his plans to launch The Players' Tribune, an
online media platform providing athletes with the opportunity to share their unfiltered thoughts and opinions without
relying on sports journalists and social media. As a high-profile athlete, Jeter understood that other athletes share similar
concerns regarding how the media interprets their remarks
and decisions and thus wanted to offer not only them, but
also the fans, unbiased storytelling.

"I do think fans deserve more than 'no comments' or 'I don't
knows,'" Jeter wrote in a letter introducing his idea. "Those
simple answers have always stemmed from a genuine concern that any statement, any opinion or detail, might be distorted. I have a unique perspective. Many of you saw me after
that final home game, when the enormity of the moment
hit me. I'm not a robot. Neither are the other athletes who
at times might seem unapproachable. We all have emotions.
We just need to be sure our thoughts will come across the
way we intend."

The announcement of The Players' Tribune made Jeter's
decision to publicize his retirement via social media more
clear: He had wanted to test the market for athlete-pro-
duced content, as well as introduce an alternative method

for announcing a retirement, both of which were integral in ensuring the success of his newly introduced venture. Jeter developed his plan of attack for The Players' Tribune well before the public was aware. By initially testing the market with his own Facebook post, Jeter saw the buzz it created among the fans and the benefits of him explaining the decision in his own words, without journalistic interpretation, hoping other athletes would follow suit.

Up until then, athletes were restricted in terms of forms of media to express themselves. Before there was social media, they had to rely on sports journalists to relay their thoughts and opinions. With Twitter and Facebook, athletes can share content directly with fans but can also be restricted by character limits and fears of "oversharing" on platforms that are meant to entertain. But using The Players' Tribune, athletes are able to discuss a wide variety of serious topics, ranging from mental health issues to gun violence, in their own words. Jeter used his own personal experiences with the media to provide athletes with an innovative approach to spreading their message, putting the power of the pen in the hands of the most powerful athletes in the world.

While Jeter was the main primary investor for his own company, Legendary Entertainment founder and former CEO Thomas Tull believed in the platform and put forth an undisclosed amount in funding, in addition to providing the star athlete with business advice. Tull's experience in the media industry, coupled with Jeter's legacy as an athlete, boosted The Players' Tribune's credibility. Just one year after announcement of the site, The Players' Tribune raised $15 million in Series B funding. Appropriately, many of the investors were professional athletes.

The Players' Tribune primarily serves athletes, providing them with an open forum to express themselves in, which is why Jeter wanted more athletes to back the venture. Jeter's wish came true when former NBA star Kobe Bryant invested a "significant amount" of funding in The Players' Tribune through his venture capital firm, Bryant Stibel Investments, in October 2015. As one of the faces of the NBA, Bryant was on Jeter's radar from the start.

"I asked Kobe to get involved from the beginning and contribute content," Jeter explained in a joint Forbes interview with Bryant on Oct. 27, 2015. "Later, after having a full understanding of what we were doing, he wanted to get more involved in the business. Besides being a phenomenal athlete, mentor and leader on the court, he's a respected voice and figure in the global sports community."

For Bryant, investing in The Players' Tribune was an easy decision to make. Playing in Los Angeles, ranked the second-largest sports market in North America by Nielsen,

Bryant understood what it was like to be scrutinized by the media and believed in the model to give athletes an opportunity to say what was on their minds without their thoughts being filtered through the media.

"I believe we are at the start of a revolution when it comes to people owning their stories and using them to build their businesses," Bryant told Forbes. "The Players' Tribune is just the beginning and I wanted to be a part of what Derek and his team have started to build."

Similarly to Jeter's announcement, Bryant decided to publicize his retirement plans through a written piece rather than a press conference. About a month into the 2015-16 NBA season, and a month after Bryant invested in Jeter's venture, The Players' Tribune published Bryant's retirement piece. Written as a poem addressed to "Basketball," the piece attracted 1 million unique views in the first two hours of posting. At the time, The Players' Tribune averaged 2 million unique views *per month*. Reaching half of the monthly average in less than two hours, Bryant's piece crashed the site and remains The Players' Tribune most read page.

Bryant is not the only NBA star to invest in the digital media platform and use it to make a big career announcement. As previously mentioned, Jeter approached Kevin Durant to join

The Players' Tribune team in September 2015, and Durant willingly invested in the platform.

"I look up to Derek, and I look forward to working with him to build a place where we athletes can have our say and feel safe that nothing will be distorted. I think that in the end, if fans get the chance to find out who we really are as people, we'll all feel a lot better about the games we love," Durant said in the press release.

Just 11 months later, Durant penned his infamous "My Next Chapter," announcing his decision to leave Oklahoma City for Silicon Valley to reach his full potential as both a basketball player and an investor.

The Players' Tribune is a perfect example of how an entrepreneur can set their venture up for success. Jeter conceived the idea for the platform based on his own personal experiences and what he identified as a need for professional athletes, as well as a want among sports fans. Jeter tested the waters of his own venture by "teasing" the platform with his Facebook retirement post, ensuring that a publication like that would generate enough buzz within the sports community and fan base. Jeter primed The Players' Tribune for success by analyzing the market and filling a void for athletes.

* * *

An NBA point guard carries a lot of responsibilities on his shoulders. Not only is he responsible for calling plays and directing players on the offensive side, but he must also be the team's best passer, capable of threading the ball between defenders to find the open man.

Each decision he makes has associated risks with it. If he passes the ball, a defender can intercept it and control possession. If he shoots the ball, it could miss and result in a defender securing the rebound. If he holds on to the ball too long, a defender can step up and strip the ball from him. No matter what, he always risks turning the ball over—which is why Steph Curry always has a plan B before putting himself in sticky in-game situations.

When the Golden State Warriors brought on former NBA 2x MVP Steve Nash as a developmental coach in 2015, his main job was to refine Steph Curry's on-court play. At the time, Curry was just coming off a career year during which he secured his first NBA championship and MVP status, but the Warriors' coaching staff believed he still had more room for growth. Nash mentored the star player, providing him with on-court advice.

"One thing he has taught me is that you always have an out," Curry told ESPN in a December 2015 interview.

Nash's advice relates to Curry's need to run through several different scenarios in his head before making a play. For every decision he makes on the court, Curry should consider a backup plan just in case a defender jumps in at the last second to deter his primary plan of attack. But the advice is not limited to the basketball court. Despite being a multimillionaire, Curry has added a side project to his playing career: launching his own startup while playing down the road from Silicon Valley.

In 2015, Curry co-founded Slyce, originally a social media platform designed specifically for athletes, which later changed to a brand ambassador management tool, with his former college basketball teammate, Bryant Barr. While talking to his former teammate, Barr wondered why Curry's social media presence declined once his popularity grew.

"We started talking about why, and he said it was mostly just a pain in the butt," Barr said in an interview with GeekWire. In a separate interview with SportTechie, Barr added, "He and I talked to guys in the league, not just the NBA but other leagues as well, and it turns out it was an industry-wide problem."

The conversation between the two former Davidson teammates continued until they arrived at the idea of Slyce, a company mainly focused on offering athletes a unique and fun way to engage with their fans through a more direct manner than traditional social media. Slyce also allows athletes to access all of their social media accounts in one place and share content directly to several different platforms at the same time, an easier method of keeping their fans up to date.

Curry's reputation as an NBA all-star brought authenticity to the newly formed platform. Within the first few months of the company's existence, Slyce recruited 10 athletes to use the platform for posting on their social media accounts. Additionally, several athletes, such as Atlanta Hawks Kent Bazemore, hosted live Q&As on the app, providing fans with even more direct engagements with star athletes.

Similar to LeBron James' involvement with Blaze Pizza, Curry was a marketing powerhouse for Slyce. Curry appeared in the season three premiere of the HBO show Ballers, which aired on July 23, 2017. During his one-minute cameo, Curry rocked a Slyce t-shirt and even suggested to the show's protagonist, played by Dwayne Johnson, that they "could even talk some business, too; you know my Slyce digital media company."

"Steph did an awesome job of being able to pull us in," Barr said to GeekWire about the Ballers appearance. "Those are the things that make it unique to work with someone like Steph."

But unlike James, Curry offers more than just marketability to the brand. He is described as a "thought leader" by Barr, and when Slyce faced stagnation in user growth rate and usage, Curry had an "out" to ensure Slyce's longevity.

During the summer of 2017, Barr noticed an increase in difficulty of getting celebrities to consistently engage with the app. To combat this issue, Barr once again turned to his co-founder for ideas. With endorsement deals with companies such as Under Armour, Infiniti, and Muscle Milk, Curry is required to promote these brands monthly on social media, which sparked his plan B for Slyce. Instead of having celebrities and athletes as the main focal point for Slyce, Curry suggested that the platform should pivot and reposition itself as a brand ambassador management platform.

The platform now tailors itself to help companies manage their brand ambassador programs by providing data analytics to better help brands track their ambassadors' performance and value. Curry's realization that Slyce's technology could also be used to collect data, such as post engagement, on specific pieces of content, coupled with the lack of interest from athletes outside of the NBA to engage with Slyce, motivated Curry to change the direction of his company.

But why does an athlete with a $200 million contract need other projects? According to Slyce's former Chief Product

Officer Jason Mayden, the answer relates to professional athletes' desire to continue to be innovative not only on the field but also in the outside world.

"What we have seen thus far is that there has been a huge interest from athletes to explore opportunities in Silicon Valley, because they understand their power beyond the court or field," Mayden explained to SportTechie. "Athletes are now sitting on boards of companies in advisement roles. They use their position to help startups innovate and grow. Innovation is at their core, and they are beginning to take the next step from physical products to digital."

At its inception, Slyce offered a new platform for athletes to engage more directly with their fans. However, Slyce failed to gain traction within the professional athlete community. Instead of throwing in the towel on something both Curry and Barr worked so hard to create, Curry thought back to what Coach Nash told him on the court and came up with an out for his off-court endeavors. Under a new direction, Slyce lives on, striving to provide brands the necessary resources and data analytics to effectively manage brand ambassador programs.

* * *

Hesitation to innovate often derives from fear of failure. Those who are risk-averse will shy away from innovative practices, continuing to rely on traditional business methods. But just because there is risk associated with a decision does not mean you should not go through with it.

While The Players' Tribune may be more well-known then Slyce, the stories of Jeter and Curry both highlight important factors that corporations and individuals must consider when engaging in innovative practices. Even before Jeter announced his business venture, the former Yankee positioned The Players' Tribune for success with a thought-out plan: first announcing his retirement on social media, introducing the concept that athletes can share stories and career-altering announcements through their own words, and then creating a digital platform months later for athletes to do just that.

Since his retirement post on Facebook, Jeter has been followed by more and more athletes taking this route, by using The Players' Tribune to explain career decisions that may get lost in translation through traditional press conferences. The risk associated with his venture was mitigated by the fact that Jeter himself was an athlete and recognized that other athletes would appreciate a platform able to promote this type of dialogue between professional athletes and sports fans. Jeter recognized that the consumer base of sports fans wanted more from athletes than just press conferences and tweets, and coupled that with athletes' desire to bypass journalists and deliver their thoughts and opinions on topics in a more direct and personal manner.

By understanding consumers' needs and effectively incorporating them into your product or service, you can diminish the risk involved with an innovative concept. If your innovative product or service addresses target consumers' needs and fills a gap in a market, consumers will be more likely to try it, despite it being a foreign idea.

For Steph Curry, the risk of Slyce failing to be attractive to professional athletes became a reality. Unlike Jeter, Curry had not fully tested the market among professional athletes and had overestimated the number of athletes willing to engage on this platform. While keeping social media accounts up to date was an industrywide problem in the eyes of Curry and Barr, the initial iteration of Slyce failed to address this issue and did not generate the buzz among professional athletes that Curry had hoped.

Yet instead of giving up on this innovative platform, Curry simply adapted his plan of attack, shifting its primary service from an athlete's message board to an analytics platform for brand ambassadors. Slyce initially failed due to its lack of popularity among both consumers—the sports fans—and content producers—athletes. The app failed to deliver a perceived benefit to fans and athletes that social media platforms did not already deliver. By understanding that there was not a market for a platform like this, Curry found an out by repositioning his company to appeal to businesses managing brand ambassadors.

Don't let risks stop you from pursuing that innovative idea. If you do your homework in understanding the market, evaluating consumers' wants and needs, and developing an out, you can reduce that level of uncertainty and position your innovative ideas for success.

CHAPTER 8

TURNING FAILURE INTO SUCCESS

"There is no innovation and creativity without failure. Period."

—*BRENE BROWN*

Every year, millions of parents sign their kids up for their first-ever organized sports league. While kids believe they are playing these sports for fun, their parents do so to allow their children to develop valuable skills. Whether it's soccer, T-ball, or basketball, youth sports offer children the opportunity to develop lifelong skills that extend beyond the playing field.

Being exposed to organized sports at an early age allows children to understand the value of teamwork, strengthen their perseverance, and experience healthy competition. Before every game, my high school lacrosse coach would ask us, "How will you respond to a bit of adversity?" encouraging us not to play with our heads hanging down when things did not go our way. I did not realize it then, but he was not coaching us for lacrosse. He was coaching us for life.

The skills developed through participation in sports translate directly to the entrepreneurial climate of corporate innovation. By promoting competition, individuals understand what it takes to be better than your opponent. In sports, practice makes perfect, but in business, one must innovate in order to gain that competitive edge.

Sports teaches you how to overcome adversity and determine how to respond to events that challenge you. If the other team scores two goals in the opening minute, are you going to play on your heels for the rest of the game, or are you going to respond with goals of your own?

Similarly, in business, you should not let past failures discourage you from pursuing your venture. And perhaps the most important takeaway from sports that translates to the business world is the importance of teamwork and the understanding that if everyone does what they are capable of doing, the company will be in a better position to innovate and succeed in the future.

* * *

Yankee legend Yogi Berra famously once said, "Baseball is 90% mental. The other half is physical."

While the math in the quote does fail to add up, the idea behind it is something every baseball player and most professional athletes in general understand and have to learn to deal with. For former MLB player Shawn Green, that lesson was learned after three full seasons with the Toronto Blue Jays.

Drafted as Toronto's first-round pick in the 1991 MLB amateur draft, Green was expected to make an immediate impact on the Blue Jay's lineup. Green received a signing bonus of $725,000, one of the highest signing bonuses at the time. But it wasn't until Green signed a six-year $84 million contract with the LA Dodgers in 2000 that his mentality interfered with his physical performance.

After hitting 42 home runs with a .309 batting average in his last season with Toronto, Green struggled in his first year as a Dodger, hitting just 24 home runs—his lowest output since his rookie season—with a .269 batting average. These are not the stats that fans wanted to see their $14 million-a-year player produce. Green tried too hard to prove to his new fans that he could replicate the stats he had in Toronto and justify his new contract, and his struggles held him out of the starting lineup.

"I had this month on the bench, and that was the time I said, 'I could sit here and pout, or I can try to make changes.' That's what I did, and I think that's the best thing that happened," Green admitted to Dave Meltzer in an interview from the podcast The Playbook.

Green implemented a series of changes to his routine, including practicing meditation to clear his mind and refocus on what was important.

"There were issues with my swing that really bothered me so I said, 'I'm just gonna break it all apart, and I'm gonna change my focus and really try to be in the moment,'" Green told Meltzer. "It's so hard in baseball, because you look at the scoreboard, and it's all about what you did in that season."

The new approach worked, as Green bashed a franchise-record 49 home runs for the Dodgers during the 2001 season while also raising his batting average by .03 points.

"To have some adversity that resets it and makes you say, 'You know what, I need to make some changes,' there isn't a better way to get out of your own way, to break everything apart and say, 'I'm going to rebuild.' For my swing and approach and my focus and mentality from meditation, [I told myself], 'I'm going to break everything apart and start over from scratch.'"

Green adapted this approach to his post-baseball career. A majority of athletes struggle following their professional careers, unsure how to fill the void left from what they've spent their entire life working on. Some athletes find themselves going back to the game, either as a coach or a broadcaster. Others play golf five times a week. But Green—he truly broke everything apart from his baseball career, putting it behind him and starting a new career from scratch.

"As a professional athlete, I think it's consistent among all the different sports, you want to get that set-for-life contract, and I had that, and you think that 'I'm just going to ride off into the sunset'; you have these visions of what your post-playing career will be," Green described. "I had all of these things I wanted to do, like spend time with my family. But what you don't realize is that you've put your entire being into a career, and it's really hard to have nothing after that."

While many retired athletes choose a relaxing, golf-filled life to fill the void, Green had no interest in doing so and instead turned to one of his other passions: technology. Similarly to Carmelo Anthony, Green was always interested in technology as a player. Despite playing in an age when wearable technologies and virtual reality were not present in sports,

Green discovered a passion for technology, reading coding books during spring training. While, admittedly, Green did not finish many of the books he read, his interest in software stuck with him following his retirement from baseball.

Unlike Anthony, Green decided to turn this interest into a company, knowing that he needed something other than golf to keep his post-baseball life occupied. Inspired by current athletes' use of social media platforms such as Facebook and Twitter, Green, along with business partner Brendon Kensel, launched Jock Talk in April 2012. A social media platform dedicated to athletes, Jock Talk gives athletes an additional medium to share their thoughts and engage in two-way communication with fans.

"I launched Jock Talk to enable better communication between athletes and fans, as well as provide athletes with an opportunity to generate income and awareness for the causes they care about," Green explained to Venture Beat.

Through its online platform, athletes were compensated for posting content on their profiles; they could easily donate the money to charities of their choosing while also encouraging the fans to donate. While the idea had potential, however, the company itself was unsuccessful. There is little to no information readily available explaining why the business failed—according to Kensel's LinkedIn profile, Jock Talk was shut down in December 2013—but it can be inferred from a quote off the podcast that the failure had to do with the team dynamic of the company.

"I was involved in some startups that didn't work," Green ambiguously mentioned to Meltzer. "It's frustrating because, especially as the guy who has the bigger bank account, it gets stressful, because you have to burn every month and make decisions, and finally you get to the point where you can't keep up."

Instead of tossing in the towel after Jock Talk's failure, Green stuck with his desire to become an entrepreneur, continuing his meditation and clearing his mind for a new idea. Similarly to his approach with his swing, Green started from scratch and launched a new venture in 2014: Greenfly. As a subscription-based software platform, Greenfly allows brands to invite a selected network of influencers to create videos, photos, and other forms of content. Brands are then able to review the submitted content, provide feedback, and release it to a wider network of ambassadors to post on their social media accounts.

When determining Greenfly's business strategy, Green took another lesson learned from his baseball career and applied to his new venture: the importance and appreciation of a team. Throughout his playing career, Green noted that he would rather be the Robin to the team's Batman than be his team's star player. With the Blue Jays, Green served as Carlos Delgado's sidekick, allowing Delgado the stardom so Green could focus on his own play. But when the Dodgers signed him, Green suddenly had to step into the spotlight and be the face of the franchise, an added pressure that could explain his early struggles in LA.

"I was always the type that, even as a player—I didn't want to be 'the guy' on the team, I wanted to be someone's wingman," Green admitted to Meltzer. "It's the same in business: I like to be the wingman. I have a great CEO running Greenfly; he is the guy that I rely on, and he bounces stuff off of me. And we're both working more than full time, but I like to be that. And we have to have the team that we do and rely on them and really rely on them to do their job well and give them the tools they need to be successful."

Green didn't want the title of CEO. Aware of his own strengths and weaknesses, Green knew he needed a strong businessperson whom he trusted to direct the company's vision. So, he called up his cousin Daniel Kirschner, who, at the time, was serving as a senior vice president at the popular video game developer Activision Blizzard.

Greenfly debuted its software and worked with the Toronto Blue Jays and Sportsnet, a Canadian sports broadcasting company, at first. Yet similarly to an athlete's rookie season, during the first few years, Greenfly had its fair share of ups and downs, forcing Green to draw on his past experience as an MLB player to maintain his confidence in the company.

"I think baseball, of all the sports, is probably the most in [that you] go through the most slumps...as a baseball player; you feel like you're never going to get a hit again," Green said. "There are days you'll say, 'I can grab someone from the stands, and they have a better chance of getting a hit than you.' On the flip side, I was very streaky and when I get hot, I was the hottest guy on the planet and couldn't get out. And it's exactly the same in an early-stage company: You get this momentum; you get this energy, and you just learn—I guess it's kind of like surfing; the set of waves is going to come in, and you just got to be prepared for when these waves come in. You just have to ride them."

One of the biggest waves that Green had the opportunity to ride was an acceptance into the Dodgers' accelerator program's second cohort in the summer of 2016, granting the new entrepreneur the chance to build his company with his former MLB team. Despite holding the franchise record for most home runs in a season, it was not Green's past performance as an athlete that captured the attention of Dodgers CFO Tucker Kain. Just like how baseball executives evaluate players, the Dodgers Accelerator team did not care about what Green did in the past: They were focused on what his future held.

"It was a fantastic bonus," Kain told the LA Times. "It just so happens that Shawn is a fantastic entrepreneur that has built an incredible company. Shawn being a former player is icing on the cake."

While working under the Dodgers Accelerator, Kain and the rest of the Dodgers' team guided Greenfly through its Series A funding round, raising a total investment of $6.2 million.

In addition to securing funding, the Dodgers Accelerator provided Greenfly with contacts that were crucial to the company's growth. Talks with MiLB—Minor League Baseball— quickly developed into a partnership between the startup and the league; starting for the 2017 season, Greenfly would provide its services for the league's "It's Fun to be a Fan" marketing campaign. Fans were able to send in their own photos and videos explaining why they think it's fun to be a fan of a minor league team in order to increase post engagement on social media platforms. According to the MiLB marketing department, the 20 most-engaged posts from the 2017 season were curated through Greenfly's system.

Greenfly also lent its help to the club that invested its resources and tools into its development. To hype up their fans for the 2016 MLB playoffs, the Dodgers enlisted Greenfly to collect fan videos expressing support for the team, making it easy for the team's social media department to accumulate, review, and post the fan-generated content in one place.

"If I were to do it all on my own, it would not have been as successful," Dodgers social media coordinator Matt Mesa admitted to the LA Times.

A successful 2017, made in part through Greenfly's development within the Dodgers Accelerator, led to a hot start for Greenfly's 2018 season. On Jan. 25, 2018, Greenfly announced the closing of its Series B round of funding, which was led by tech venture capital firm Alpha Edison, raising an additional $8.5 million to be used to further develop Greenfly's existing technology and expand its team of employees.

"Alpha Edison joining the Greenfly team further validates the importance of what we have built and the enormous market demand for the Greenfly technology to simplify the digital content creation and distribution process," Kirschner said.

* * *

There are several parallels between Green's playing career and experience as an entrepreneur that can explain his success in both fields. For one, Green learned the importance of living in the moment rather than focusing on the past. Through mindfulness and meditation, Green realized he needed to change his approach to the plate and adapt his swing in order to return to the type of player he was earlier in his career. After scrapping Jock Talk, Green shifted his focus onto a new idea rather than kicking himself over a poor past performance.

Additionally, Green learned the importance of teamwork from his baseball career. Cognizant of his personal strengths and weaknesses, Green viewed himself as a sidekick or a wingman and needed someone he could trust as the company's CEO. By hiring someone he grew up with as Greenfly's CEO, Green could concentrate on the company's vision while Kirschner dealt with the complicated business practices that Green did not feel comfortable with; Green used this dynamic as a learning experience.

Perhaps the biggest takeaway from his baseball career was Green's realization that slumps occur, but so do hot streaks. It's important for entrepreneurs to face adversity early on, and it is even more important for them to learn how to overcome adversity. Similarly, corporate innovators cannot fear failure and instead should view failures as learning experiences.

Just like in baseball, an individual's future potential is not always based on their past performance. In Green's case, he revitalized his entrepreneurial career by not only identifying a strong idea, but also bringing in a strong team to turn that good idea into a great business in Greenfly.

Jock Talk was a shaky start to Green's entrepreneurial career, but that did not prevent him from starting another, more successful startup. If he let the failure of Jock Talk get the best of him, he would not have been able to experience the success of Greenfly.

"In baseball I learned that you're never as good as your greatest streak; you're never as bad as your biggest slump, and it's completely analogous to this type of experience," Green mused.

CHAPTER 9

LESSONS FROM
THE FIELD

———

"There's a way to do it better—find it."

—*THOMAS EDISON*

On Feb. 16, 2018, Fox News journalist Laura Ingraham came under fire when she responded to LeBron James' criticism of Donald Trump with the now infamous quote:

"It's always unwise to seek political advice from someone who gets paid $100 million a year to bounce a ball," Ingraham claimed. "Keep the political comments to yourselves. ... Shut up and dribble."

"Shut up and dribble."

A phrase directed at the athlete to discourage him from speaking out about topics and issues other than sports. A phrase intended to be malicious in an effort to discredit James' opinion. A phrase suggesting that because he is an athlete, James is unable to express his own thoughts and opinions on a subject outside sports.

Labels are constrictive and fail to relay the whole picture. While James is perhaps the most recognizable athlete on the planet, he is—to borrow from his Instagram photo posted shortly after Ingraham's comments—"more than an athlete."

He is a father of three kids.

He is a philanthropist.

He is a businessman.

And just because James' primary career is playing professional basketball, that does not discredit his thoughts, opinions, or actions—whether it's a political comment or a business decision. As one of the people leading charges in the recent trend of NBA stars investing in startups, James exemplifies his role as a thought leader among his peers.

And it is not just James. It is every sports organization, athlete, or sports owner mentioned in this book that has broken this stereotype and gone beyond their stereotypical role in sports. In a traditionally "lazy" industry regarding innovation, these individuals and organizations have embraced technology and taken advantage of the shifts in consumer behavior due to the Digital Age. Whether you are an aspiring entrepreneur working on your own startup or a corporation struggling to innovate internally, there are lessons in the stories of these athletes and teams on how to embrace innovation and successfully do so externally.

* * *

The Los Angeles Dodgers were primed to be the first professional sports team to launch an accelerator program just based on the ownership group that orchestrated the $2 billion sale. The Guggenheim Baseball Management group consisted of experienced investors such as Guggenheim Partner CEO Mark Walter, Eldridge Industries CEO Todd Boehly, and Magic Johnson.

Similarly, the Philadelphia 76ers' current ownership group, now branded as Harris Blitzer Sports & Entertainment, purchased the team for a reported $280 million in 2011. The investment backgrounds of 76ers Principal Owner Joshua Harris, co-founder of the public equity firm Apollo Global

Management, and his co-owner David Blizter, the Global Head of Blackstone's Tactical Opportunities group, justified the organization's decision to follow suit and create an accelerator program of its own.

In both cases, having experienced, wealthy investors running your sports organization and investing in startups was not enough. Before they started accepting applications, they had to create credibility within the startup ecosystem and build their entrepreneurial brand, which starts with who will lead the innovation team.

CB Insights CEO Anand Sanwal offers his own advice in selecting an individual to lead relationships with entrepreneurs and startups.

"You want someone who, especially if you're looking to build relationships with entrepreneurs, who's going to listen to entrepreneurs," Sanwal advised. "Who is going to be empathetic. Who's going to be able to help them."

For the first two years of its existence, the Dodgers Accelerator program was operated by Dodgers CFO Tucker Kain. However, when the program rebranded itself to Global Sports Venture Studio, Tim Katt, with a background as a venture capitalist, was named managing director.

The 76ers Innovation Lab's external selection of Seth Berger demonstrates the qualities and traits a firm wants to lead its accelerator program. Not only did Berger have an existing relationship with 76ers CEO Scott O'Neill, but Berger also has experience as an entrepreneur, building his AND1 brand in numerous ways, from selling apparel out of his car to Vince Carter wearing his shoes while winning the 2000 NBA Slam Dunk Contest.

Berger runs the 76ers Innovation Lab with a very hands-on approach, as he works closely with each startups' teams to provide them with the necessary resources to succeed. With young, inexperienced entrepreneurs like Dylan Elder, Berger recognized his responsibility to teach Elder about business, assisting him in rebranding his company and adapting Monster Roster's business model.

Which leads to my second point as to why Berger is the model leader for accelerator programs. Once the applications are received, the next task is to identify the potential winners. And while some may believe that it is in the organization's best interest to select the ideas believed to have the most potential, Berger stresses that the most important consideration is the people behind the idea.

Again looking at Elder as an example, Berger saw an entrepreneur who was far from his full potential due to Elder's lack of business knowledge. Additionally, Berger viewed Elder as a hard-working individual who is also easily coachable, evidenced by Elder reworking his pitch after Berger initially tore it apart. To succeed as an accelerator program, the leader of the team must be able to identify winners by prioritizing the person over the idea and then applying their own past entrepreneurial success to mentoring those entrepreneurs.

* * *

Not every sports organization is owned by groups controlled by career investors, and accelerator programs are not the only answer to corporate innovation. Partnerships require less capital and less "coaching" from the organizations and are used by sports owners, such as Ted Leonsis, to incorporate new technologies into their teams.

Coming from a tech background, Leonsis does not fear innovation; he embraces it. His approach to handling strategic partnerships should be emulated by business leaders in all industries. Leonsis will do anything to improve his teams' performances and does so by putting his skin in the game.

From the moment he put on the virtual reality goggles, Leonsis knew that STRIVR had something special. Leonsis also knew that no other NBA, NHL, or WNBA had access to technology like this. As a leader rather than a follower, Leonsis did not fear the fact that no other team in his leagues were partnering with STRIVR. Instead, Leonsis recognized the value of STRIVR's asset and the increase in value of being the first teams to wield this technology. Leonsis wanted to provide his teams with a competitive advantage offered nowhere else. Leonsis' willingness to invest, coupled with Washington Capitals coaches and players welcoming the new technology with open minds, gave the team an advantage in practice, helping the franchise capture its first Stanley Cup.

When approaching partnerships, it is important for both parties to feel respected by the terms of the deal. Sanwal offered his own insight on why it is not enough for corporations to just offer free advice or branding in exchange for access to a startup's product or service.

"It's, one, an indication that it's not a big enough deal for you to internally get a champion for, or even for you to become a champion for. And, two, that you don't think highly enough of the startup to solve it. So you're wasting your time and the startup's time. So, again, 'skin in the game' comes down to money," Sanwal said.

If a corporation wants to partner with a startup, it better make sure the startup understands how much it means to the corporation. Looking back at Belch's experiences talking to NFL teams, several teams expected STRIVR's services to be offered for free on the basis of the team's brand, leaving Belch feeling disrespected. As it goes, those teams who did not put their skin in the game missed out on an opportunity to improve athletic performance through innovative technology, while the teams that did offer capital reaped the benefits of the competitive edge.

Furthermore, Leonsis' decisions regarding partnerships have a common goal of increasing the value of the Monumental brand for the consumers. Whether it's virtual reality training to increase team performance, interactive mobile streams, or involvement in the eSports industry, Leonsis positions his brand as one that puts the consumer first. A better team means a better chance at winning a championship, which leads to happier fans and more bodies in the stadium. In the acquisition of Team Liquid, Leonsis identified an emerging trend in the sports industry and recognized its potential to be a global phenomenon; he gave a reason for eSports fans to consume content on Monumental Sports Network.

Never fear being the first to do something. That's the basis of innovation.

* * *

When practicing corporate innovation, failure will occur. Great ideas do not always become great businesses. But, rather than getting discouraged by failure, all innovative individuals should embrace the trait of overcoming adversity and view failure as a learning experience. When failure happens, individuals must analyze mistakes and devise how to not repeat them.

Investors and entrepreneurs alike will not always strike gold on their business decisions. Things will never go exactly as planned. Startups will fail; investments will be lost. But what separates successful entrepreneurs and investors from failures is their response to adversity.

Elder thought his opportunity to run a successful startup was crushed by DraftKing and FanDuel's announcement banning lineup selling. However, Elder worked alongside Berger to adapt Monster Roster's business model, turning it into a lineup optimizer tool and allowing it to be utilized by daily fantasy sports users.

Elder could have easily thrown in the towel and returned to school. But he had already worked so hard to reach this point, and under the direction of a mentor he trusted, he was able to shift Monster Roster and see its growth continue since the legalization of sports betting.

Curry and Green have similar stories as athlete-entrepreneurs, struggling to create buzz and attention for their first projects. But Curry had an out, pivoting the company to a new direction that he perceived brought more value to potential users. For Green, it was about recognizing why the first startup failed and surrounding himself with experienced businesspeople that he could trust to launch his second project, Greenfly, which ultimately was accepted into the Dodgers' accelerator program.

Innovation requires failure. Do not let the fear of failure discourage you.

* * *

The presence of the modern-day athlete extends far beyond the field on which they play. Athletes such as James, Jeter, and Durant have redefined what it means to be a high-profile athlete. Not only do they excel on the field, but they are also succeeding in their ventures off the field.

Rather than sticking to just basketball, James invested in Blaze Pizza and quickly saw it become the fastest-growing restaurant chain in U.S. history. Durant based a career-altering decision not only on factors to increase his on-court accomplishments but also on ones to boost his investment portfolio. As investors, Durant's and James' willingness to learn and listen to their mentors put them in a position to become successful investors. Once they checked their egos at the door, it was no longer former MVP LeBron James requesting a meeting with Blaze Pizza, but potential investor LeBron James wanting to learn more about the business.

And for The Players' Tribune, Jeter reduced the risk of failure by identifying an existing need among athletes and testing the platform through his own retirement announcement to see how sports fans would consume the content. In the end, Jeter primed The Players' Tribune for success because he of all people knew that athletes wanted an outlet to share their personal stories directly to fans and that fans deserved this more unfiltered access to an athlete's mind.

* * *

The great thing about innovation is that it will never dissipate. Innovation is required for a society to move forward and progress. Innovation is required in order for sports teams to improve team performance and boost relationships with fans in the digital age. Innovation is required for corporations to provide consumers with what they want, before they even know they want it.

Innovation is a never-ending process. Just trust it.

ACKNOWLEDGEMENTS

———

First, I would like to thank my parents whose unconditional love and support helped ease the writing process. Thank you for continuously supporting my interests, allowing me to pursue my pasions and calming me down when writing became stressful. You guys served as my main source of motivation and I thank you for that.

I would also like to thank my sister, Marisa Cowdry, and my brother, Nick Hoffman, for showing me that taking chances and pursuing your dreams is not crazy. You guys are rockstars and I look up to both of you.

Thank you to all of the wonderful individuals who dedicated their time to talk to me and teach me more about this topic. Thank you Derek Belch, Seth Berger, Jimmy Lynn, Rick

Wetzel and Eric Woolworth for taking time out of their busy schedule to answer my questions—without your input this book would not exist.

Thank you to all of my Georgetown friends who patiently listened to me talking about writing a book for a ten-month period. Whether it was sharing my excitement for finishing a chapter or understanding my frustrations after a 10-hour writing binge in Lau, your everlasting support kept me motivated and determined to accomplish my goal.

Thank you Eric Koester for making the impossible possible. Heading into the course I had zero idea how I was going to write a book in less than a year. But your enthusiasm was contagious and seeing your excitement about publishing student authors just made me want to write a book even more. You and the rest of the New Degree Press team, especially Brian Bies, made the task less daunting and provided the necessary resources for me to succeed throughout the process—thank you.

Finally, I would like to personally thank Dylan Elder for inspiring me to write this book. Your dedication to your company is remarkable and your story needed to be heard. I cannot begin to express how thankful I am for your contributions to this book. I am excited to attend your college graduation in 2025.

APPENDIX

Introduction:

Colletti, Ned. "Six Years Ago, the Bankrupt Los Angeles Dodgers Were in a Very Different Place." SI.com. October 4, 2017. Accessed August 29, 2018. https://www.si.com/mlb/2017/10/06/ned-colletti-big-chair-book-excerpt-los-angeles-dodgers-bankruptcy-frank-mccourt.

Solomon, Brian. "$2 Billion Dodgers Sale Tops List Of Most Expensive Sports Team Purchases Ever." Forbes. March 30, 2012. Accessed September 1, 2018. https://www.forbes.com/sites/briansolomon/2012/03/29/2-billion-dodgers-sale-tops-list-of-most-expensive-sports-team-purchases-ever/#307d3f9b4206.

Chapter 1:

Sanwal, Anand. "Corporate Innovation Trends Webinar." *CB Insights (video), January 15, 2016. https://www.youtube.com/ watch?time_continue=922&v=l13xWfViQLk.*

Bubenzer-Paim, Andreas. "Innovation Isn't Just For Startups: How Big Companies Can Tap Their Creative Power." Forbes. April 19, 2018. Accessed October 09, 2018. https://www.forbes.com/ sites/forbestechcouncil/2018/04/19/innovation-isnt-just-for-startups-how-big-companies-can-tap-their-creative-power/#-7d93a02d686b.

Colletti, Ned. "Six Years Ago, the Bankrupt Los Angeles Dodgers Were in a Very Different Place." SI.com. October 4, 2017. Accessed August 29, 2018. https://www.si.com/mlb/2017/10/06/ ned-colletti-big-chair-book-excerpt-los-angeles-dodgers-bankruptcy-frank-mccourt.

Kennedy, John. "Disciplined Innovation: How Apple Became a $1trn Tech Giant." Siliconrepublic. August 03, 2018. Accessed August 29, 2018. https://www.siliconrepublic.com/companies/ apple-turnaround-analysis.

Lenet, Scott. "Analyzing the Spectrum of Corporate Innovation From R&D to VC." TechCrunch. April 21, 2017. Accessed

August 29, 2018. https://techcrunch.com/2017/04/21/analyz-
ing-the-spectrum-of-corporate-innovation-from-rd-to-vc/.

Ries, Eric. *The Startup Way: How Modern Companies Use Entrepreneurial Management to Transform Culture and Drive Long-
term Growth.* Portfolio Penguin, 2017.

Solomon, Yoram. "Why R&D Spending Has Almost No Correlation to Innovation." Innovation Excellence. Accessed
August 29, 2018. https://www.innovationexcellence.com/
blog/2017/11/27/why-rd-spending-has-almost-no-correlation-
to-innovation/.

Viki, Tendayi. "Why R&D Spending Is Not A Measure Of Innovation." Forbes. August 30, 2016. Accessed August 30, 2018.
https://www.forbes.com/sites/tendayiviki/2016/08/21/why-
rd-spending-is-not-a-measure-of-innovation/#1938024c77dd.

Wang, Ray. "Walkman to IPod: Business-Model Transforma-
tion." Recode. September 03, 2015. Accessed August 30, 2018.
https://www.recode.net/2015/9/3/11618292/book-excerpt-busi-
ness-model-transformation.

Weinswig, Deborah. "Deep Dive: The Evolution of Corporate
Innovation". Fung Global Retail & Technology. May 17, 2017.
Accessed September 01, 2018.https://www.fungglobalretailtech.

com/wp-content/uploads/2017/05/The-Evolution-of-Corpo-rate-Innovation-May-17_2017-DF.pdf

Chapter 2:

Alexander, Rachel. "Pollin Sells Capitals to AOL Executive; $200 Million Deal Includes Share of Wizards, MCI Center." *The Washington Post*, May 13, 1999. May 13, 1999. Accessed September 2, 2018. http://www.washingtonpost.com/wp-srv/sports/capitals/longterm/1999/sale/sale13.htm?noredirect=on.

Chacar, Aya S., and William Hesterly. "Innovations and Value Creation in Major League Baseball, 1860–2000." *Business History 46, no. 3 (July 2004): 407-38.*

"Mobile Fact Sheet." Pew Internet. February 05, 2018. Accessed September 2, 2018. http://www.pewinternet.org/fact-sheet/mobile/.

Chapter 3:

Appetize. "Appetize Launches Payment Platform Across 32 Live Nation Venues Nationwide." News release, April 6, 2015. Appetize App. https://appetizeapp.com/appetize-launches-payment-platform-across-29-live-nation-venues-nationwide-2/.

Gurnick, Ken. "Dodgers Launch Global Sports Venture Studio." MLB.com. January 8, 2018. Accessed April 2, 2018. https://

www.mlb.com/news/dodgers-launch-global-sports-venture-studio/c-264422258.

Kuo, Benjamin F. "Why The LA Dodgers Accelerator Is Combining Sports, Investment and Startups." Socal Tech. August 25, 2015. Accessed April 7, 2018. https://www.socaltech.com/why_the_la_dodgers_accelerator_is_combining_sports_investment_and_startups/s-0061617.html.

Mullin, Matt. "One Company at New Sixers Innovation Lab Can Help Make It Easier to #RaiseTheCat." PhillyVoice. July 18, 2017. Accessed April 10, 2018. https://www.phillyvoice.com/one-company-new-sixers-innovation-lab-wants-help-you-raisethecat/.

Shaikin, Bill. "Dodgers Launch Business Accelerator with Goal of Improving Fan Experience." Los Angeles Times. April 14, 2015. Accessed April 8, 2018. http://www.latimes.com/sports/dodgers/dodgersnow/la-sp-dn-dodgers-technology-business-accelerator-program-20150414-story.html.

Soper, Taylor. "Meet the 10 Startups in the Dodgers' New Sports Tech Accelerator." GeekWire. August 24, 2015. Accessed April 8, 2018. https://www.geekwire.com/2015/meet-the-10-startups-in-the-dodgers-new-sports-tech-accelerator/.

Takiff, Jonathan. "Start-ups Get an Assist from Sixers Innovation Lab." Philly. September 15, 2018. Accessed April 8, 2018. http://www2.philly.com/philly/business/technology/sixers-innovation-lab-goes-for-the-gold-20170719.html.

Wamsley, David. "Dodgers Accelerator Tech Demo Day: A View From Home Plate." Startup Grind. November 2015. Accessed April 10, 2018. https://www.startupgrind.com/blog/dodgers-accelerator-tech-demo-day-a-view-from-home-plate/.

Zerucha, Tony. "Appetize Makes Ballpark Concession Ordering Easier to Stomach." Bankless Times. June 29, 2017. Accessed October 10, 2018. https://www.banklesstimes.com/2017/06/29/appetize-makes-ballpark-concession-ordering-easier-to-stomach/.

"NoBowl Feeding System Rebrands Under New Name: Doc & Phoebe's Cat Company." Pet Age. August 8, 2017. Accessed April 10, 2018. https://www.petage.com/nobowl-feeding-system-rebrands-under-new-name-doc-phoebes-cat-company/.

Chapter 4:

Williams, David K. "The Most Valuable Business Commodity: Trust." Forbes. June 21, 2013. Accessed March 30, 2018. https://www.forbes.com/sites/davidkwilliams/2013/06/20/the-most-valuable-business-commodity-trust/#46a4e7af6500.

Chapter 5:

Allen, Scott. "D.C.'s New Entertainment and Sports Arena to Host Major ESports Competition in November." The Washington Post. March 01, 2018. Accessed April 11, 2018. https://www. washingtonpost.com/news/dc-sports-bog/wp/2018/03/01/d- c-s-new-entertainment-and-sports-arena-to-host-esports- competition-in-november/?utm_term=.3dc4dd5c8076.

Cwieka, Andrea. "Monumental Sports Network's New Play for Younger Viewers Is 'choose Your Own Adventure'." Washington Business Journal. August 15, 2017. Accessed April 11, 2018. https://www.bizjournals.com/washington/news/2017/08/15/ monumental-sports-networks-new-play-for-younger.html.

Feldman, Bruce. "'I Was Blown Away': Welcome to Football's Quarterback Revolution." FOX Sports. March 11, 2015. Accessed April 12, 2018. https://www.foxsports.com/college-football/ story/stanford-cardinal-nfl-virtual-reality-qb-training-031115.

Haberstroh, Tom. "John Wall: 'I Really Thought I Was Gonna Die'." ESPN. February 08, 2017. Accessed April 13, 2018. http:// www.espn.com/nba/story/_/page/presents5/washington-wiz- ards-virtual-reality.

Heath, Thomas. "Keys to Leonsis's Success: Networking and Dedication to Work, No Matter How Menial." The Washington

Post. February 15, 2010. Accessed April 13, 2018. http://www.washingtonpost.com/wp-dyn/content/article/2010/02/14/AR2010021402917.html.

Lieberman, David. "Peter Guber And Ted Leonsis Lead Buying Group For Esports Power Team Liquid." Deadline. September 27, 2016. Accessed April 16, 2018. https://deadline.com/2016/09/peter-guber-ted-leonsis-lead-group-buy-control-esports-team-liquid-1201826800/.

Long, Michael. "ESPORTS WEEK: In the Game—the Global Sports Industry's March towards Esports." SportsPro. February 12, 2018. Accessed October 10, 2018. http://www.sportspromedia.com/analysis/esports-week-sports-industry-competitive-gaming.

Soper, Taylor. "Dallas Cowboys Players Will Use Virtual Reality Headsets to Improve On-field Decision-making." GeekWire. June 08, 2015. Accessed April 14, 2018. https://www.geekwire.com/2015/dallas-cowboys-players-will-use-virtual-reality-headsets-to-improve-on-field-decision-making/.

Volk, Pete. "Ted Leonsis: "I Do Believe [esports] Will Be as Mainstream as Hollywood and the NBA"." The Rift Herald. November 07, 2016. Accessed April 12, 2018. https://www.riftherald.com/interviews/2016/11/7/13551520/ted-leonsis-team-liquid-interview-esports.

White, Paul. "Upon Further Review, Instant Replay a Mixed Bag."
USA Today. April 10, 2014. Accessed April 14, 2018. https://
www.usatoday.com/story/sports/mlb/2014/04/09/mlb-instant-
replay-transfer-play-ejections/7527421/.

"Capitals Announce Partnership with Kiswe." Capital's Today.
September 13, 2016. Accessed April 13, 2018. https://capitalsto-
day.monumentalsportsnetwork.com/2016/09/13/capitals-an-
nounce-partnership-with-kiswe.

"Monumental Sports & Entertainment Becomes First In NBA,
NHL and WNBA to Utilize STRIVR Labs' Virtual Reality
Technology." NHL.com. August 12, 2015. Accessed October
10, 2018. https://www.nhl.com/capitals/news/monumen-
tal-sports-entertainment-becomes-first-in-nba-nhl-and-wn-
ba-to-utilize-strivr-labs-virtual-reality-technology/c-776819.

Chapter 6:

Badenhausen, Kurt. "LeBron James-Backed Blaze Pizza Is Fastest-Growing Restaurant Chain Ever." Forbes. August 03, 2017.
Accessed March 20, 2018. https://www.forbes.com/sites/kurt-
badenhausen/2017/07/11/lebron-james-backed-blaze-pizza-is-
fastest-growing-restaurant-chain-ever/#679778ac52b2.

Dowd, Kevin. "A Look at Kevin Durant's Search for Slam Dunks
in VC." PitchBook. June 5, 2018. Accessed September 10, 2018.

https://pitchbook.com/news/articles/a-look-at-kevin-durants-search-for-slam-dunks-in-vc.

Hartnett, Tyson. "Why Athletes Go Broke And What We Can Do About It." The Huffington Post. May 05, 2015. Accessed March 22, 2018. https://www.huffingtonpost.com/tyson-hartnett/why-athletes-go-broke-and_b_6812864.html.

Henry, Zoë. "Why LeBron James Invested in This Artisanal Pizza Company." Inc.com. May 22, 2015. Accessed April 20, 2018. https://www.inc.com/zoe-henry/why-lebron-james-invested-in-this-artisanal-pizza-company.html.

Neuharth-Keusch, AJ. "Kevin Durant Delivered His Shoes via Bicycle to Customers in New York City." USA Today. June 27, 2016. Accessed September 10, 2018. https://www.usatoday.com/story/sports/nba/2016/06/27/kevin-durant-free-agent-shoes-postmates-delivery/86436974/.

Postmates. "Kevin Durant X Postmates—Score 2 Tickets to Game 2 of the NBA Finals." News release, May 31, 2018. Postmates.com. Accessed September 11, 2018. https://blog.postmates.com/kevin-durant-x-postmates-score-2-tickets-to-game-2-of-the-nba-finals-82008144d488.

Rovell, Darren. "Inside Kevin Durant's Growing Empire." ESPN. May 22, 2018. Accessed September 10, 2018. http://www.espn.

com/nba/story/_/id/23532594/how-kevin-durant-building-sil-
icon-valley-empire.

Rovell, Darren. "LeBron James Leaving McDonald's, Investing
in Pizza Franchise Blaze." ESPN. October 10, 2015. Accessed
March 20, 2018. http://www.espn.com/nba/story/_/id/13835715/
lebron-james-invest-endorse-fast-casual-pizza-franchise-
blaze.

Saltzman, Jason. "How Carmelo Anthony Is Becoming a Tech
Player." Entrepreneur. February 09, 2015. Accessed April 2,
2018. https://www.entrepreneur.com/article/242691.

Shieber, Jonathan. "Knicks Star Carmelo Anthony Launches Venture Firm." TechCrunch. July 21, 2014. Accessed April 1, 2018.
https://techcrunch.com/2014/07/21/knicks-star-carmelo-an-
thony-launches-venture-firm/.

Sullivan, Gail. "Report: LeBron James Set for $30 Million Profit
on Apple-Beats Deal." The Washington Post. June 12, 2014.
Accessed March 23, 2018. https://www.washingtonpost.com/
news/morning-mix/wp/2014/06/12/report-lebron-james-set-
for-30-million-profit-on-apple-beats-deal/?noredirect=on.

TechCrunch. "From NBA to ROI with Carmelo Anthony & Stuart Goldfarb (Melo7 Tech Partners) at TechCrunch Disrupt".

Filmed [May 2016]. YouTube video, 20:20. Posted [May 2016].
https://www.youtube.com/watch?v=t1k8r5i0Cf8.

Tepper, Fitz. "How Living in Silicon Valley Has Made Kevin Durant
a Better Investor." TechCrunch. September 19, 2017. Accessed
September 10, 2018. https://techcrunch.com/2017/09/19/how-
living-in-silicon-valley-has-made-kevin-durant-a-better-in-
vestor/.

Valverde, Miriam. "LeBron James 'all In' with Blaze Pizza." Sun
Sentinel. October 13, 2015. Accessed March 21, 2018. http://
www.sun-sentinel.com/business/consumer/fl-lebron-james-
blaze-pizza-20151013-story.html.

Chapter 7:

Connley, Courtney. "How Steph Curry Applied This Advice from
Steve Nash to Success beyond Sports." CNBC. July 12, 2017.
Accessed April 14, 2018. https://www.cnbc.com/2017/07/12/
steph-curry-applies-this-advice-from-steve-nash-to-off-
court-success.html.

DiMoro, Anthony. "Kobe Bryant And Derek Jeter Join Forces
At The Players' Tribune." Forbes. October 27, 2015. Accessed
April 13, 2018. https://www.forbes.com/sites/anthonydim-
oro/2015/10/27/kobe-bryant-and-derek-jeter-join-forces-at-
the-players-tribune/#d6508d91713e.

Jeter, Derek. "The Start of Something New." The Players' Tribune. October 1, 2014. Accessed April 13, 2018. https://www.theplayerstribune.com/en-us/articles/introducing-derek-jeter.

Kepner, Tyler. "Jeter Makes His Mark as Captain Away From the Media's Spotlight." The New York Times. April 01, 2007. Accessed April 12, 2018. https://www.nytimes.com/2007/04/01/sports/baseball/01jeter.html.

Mamiit, Aaron. "Kobe Bryant Breaks The Internet: Retirement Post Had 1 Million Clicks In First 2 Hours." Tech Times. December 02, 2015. Accessed April 13, 2018. https://www.techtimes.com/articles/112654/20151202/kobe-bryant-breaks-the-internet-retirement-post-had-1-million-clicks-in-first-2-hours.htm.

Melillo, Daniel. "Steph Curry's Slyce Co-Founders Share Inspiration And Vision For The Social Media Startup." SportTechie. March 19, 2016. Accessed April 13, 2018. https://www.sporttechie.com/steph-currys-slyce-co-founders-share-inspiration-and-vision-for-the-social-media-startup/.

McFadden, Jonathan. "NBA Star Stephen Curry Joins Tech Startup." Charlotte Observer. March 30, 2015. Accessed April 14, 2018. https://www.charlotteobserver.com/news/business/article16890329.html.

Petchesky, Barry. "Derek Jeter Denies Giving Gift Baskets To One-Night Stands." Deadspin. November 20, 2015. Accessed April 13, 2018. https://deadspin.com/derek-jeter-denies-giving-gift-baskets-to-one-night-sta-1743730919.

Smith, Chris. "Derek Jeter Opens the Door." Daily Intelligencer. September 22, 2014. Accessed April 13, 2018. http://nymag.com/daily/intelligencer/2014/09/derek-jeter-private-photos.html.

Soper, Taylor. "How Steph Curry Helped His Digital Marketing Startup Pivot and Land a Cameo in HBO's 'Ballers'." GeekWire. August 05, 2017. Accessed April 14, 2018. https://www.geekwire.com/2017/steph-curry-helped-digital-marketing-startup-pivot-land-cameo-hbos-ballers/.

Soper, Taylor. "NBA Star Steph Curry Launches Slyce, a New Startup Helping Athletes Optimize Social Media Chatter." GeekWire. March 03, 2016. Accessed April 13, 2018. https://www.geekwire.com/2016/slyce/.

Chapter 8:

Chen, I-Chun. "Greenfly Secures $6.2 Million in Funding." Bizjournals.com. November 10, 2016. Accessed April 20, 2018. https://www.bizjournals.com/losangeles/news/2016/11/10/greenfly-secures-6-2-million-in-funding.html.

Ellingson, Annlee. "L.A. Startup Raises $8.5 Million to Help Brands Get Fans to Do Their Marketing." Bizjournals.com. January 25, 2018. Accessed April 20, 2018. https://www.bizjournals.com/losangeles/news/2018/01/25/la-startup-raises-8-5-million-to-help-brands-get.html.

Kelly, Heather. "JockTalk Brings Pro-athletes and Fans Closer Together." VentureBeat. April 19, 2012. Accessed April 20, 2018. https://venturebeat.com/2012/04/19/jocktalk-demo/.

"How Minor League Baseball Is Using Club Content To Drive Fan Engagement." IEG Sponsorship. August 21, 2017. Accessed April 20, 2018. http://www.sponsorship.com/Report/2017/08/21/How-Minor-League-Baseball-Is-Using-Club-Content-To.aspx.

"Shawn Green: Battling Ego in the MLB." Interview. *Entrepreneur* (audio blog), November 28, 2017. Accessed April 20, 2018. https://www.entrepreneur.com/listen/playbook/305402.

Chapter 9:

Sanwal, Anand. "Corporate Innovation Trends Webinar." *CB Insights (video), January 15, 2016. https://www.youtube.com/watch?time_continue=922&v=l13xWfViQLk.*

11045807R00117

Made in the USA
San Bernardino, CA
02 December 2018